DO NOT REMOVE
CARDS FROM POCKET

ALLEN COUNTY PUBLIC LIBRARY

FORT WAYNE, INDIANA 46802

You may return this book to any agency, branch,
or bookmobile of the Allen County Public Library.

From Physician Shortage
to Patient Shortage

From Physician Shortage to Patient Shortage

The Uncertain Future of Medical Practice

edited by
Eli Ginzberg

Cornell University Medical College
Second Conference on Health Policy

Westview Press / Boulder and London

Conservation of Human Resources Studies in Health Policy

Copyright © 1986 by Conservation of Human Resources, Columbia University

Published in 1986 in the United States of America by Westview Press, Inc.; Frederick A. Praeger, Publisher; 5500 Central Avenue, Boulder, Colorado 80301

Library of Congress Cataloging-in-Publication Data
From physician shortage to patient shortage.
  (Conservation of human resources studies in health
policy)
  Includes index.
  1. Physicians—United States—Supply and demand.
2. Medical care—United States—Utilization.
3. Physicians—Employment—United States. I. Ginzberg,
Eli, 1911– . II. Series. [DNLM: 1. Health
Manpower—supply and distribution—United States.
2. Health Manpower—trends—United States.
W 76 F931]
RA410.7.F76 1986   331.12'9161'0973   86-13313
ISBN 0-8133-7276-3 (alk. paper)
ISBN 0-8133-7270-4 (pbk.)

Composition for this book was provided by Conservation of Human Resources.
This book was produced without formal editing by the publisher.

Printed and bound in the United States of America

∞ The paper used in this publication meets the requirements of the American National
   Standard for Permanence of Paper for Printed Library Materials Z39.48-1984.

6   5   4   3   2   1

Contents

Tables and Figures

Figures

Preface

This book contains five chapters based on papers that were prepared for the Cornell University Medical College Second Conference on Health Policy held in New York City on February 27–28, 1986, plus an introductory chapter and a summary of the discussion written by me as chairman and editor.

The title, *From Physician Shortage to Patient Shortage: The Uncertain Future of Medical Practice*, underscores two of the major changes that are operating to reshape the U.S. health care sector.

Two major contributions to the Conference have not been reproduced: the opening remarks of Dr. Frank Rhodes, the president of Cornell University, who challenged the conferees to move beyond analysis to policy formulation; and a luncheon address by the Honorable James Tallon, chairman, Health Committee, New York State Assembly, who explored the need and the potential avenues for more effective cooperation between government and the private sector in developing health policy.

As in 1985, I was greatly assisted by Dean Thomas H. Meikle, Jr., and Associate Dean Michael J. Sniffen in the planning, organization, and execution of the Conference. Theda Jensen of the associate dean's office was responsible for all of the arrangements in connection with assembling and accommodating our many out-of-town participants.

Conservation of Human Resources staff members Miriam Ostow, Howard Berliner, and, in particular, Penny Peace had the task of overseeing and coordinating the numerous steps in the development of the Conference from liaison with the authors and conferees to preparing the Conference materials and producing the final manuscript for publication. Ruth Szold Ginzberg edited the papers for publication with sensitivity and skill.

Through the early publication of this book, we hope that many individuals with an interest in health policy who were not present will profit from the opportunity to read the papers and be stimulated by the diverse themes and perceptions reflected in the summary of the discussion.

From Physician Shortage to Patient Shortage is a companion to the 1985 proceedings volume, entitled *The U.S. Health Care System: A Look to the 1990s,* published by Rowman & Allanheld.

Eli Ginzberg
Conservation of Human Resources
Columbia University

1

The Setting

Eli Ginzberg

This introductory chapter has several related objectives. It provides the rationale which underpinned the planning for the Second Cornell University Medical College Conference on Health Policy; sets the next five chapters within the framework of that planning; provides a condensed overview of the historical antecedents of the two facets of the changing health care system on which the Conference focused—the physician surplus and the looming shifts and possible declines in the demand for health care services; and serves as a ballast to Chapter 7, in which the policy directions that emerged from the Conference are summarized.

In planning for the Conference, some simplifying assumptions were established: Instead of asking whether the country has a physician surplus or was likely to confront one in the near future, we simply postulated that the term "surplus" would refer to the substantial and continuing increases in the physician supply, increases which were occurring in a period when government and employers were seeking to contain their expenditures for health care.

We also postulated that the demand for patient services, particularly hospital services, has begun to decline and that there is evidence that this trend also is true for the visits that patients are making to physicians practicing in ambulatory settings. We recognize, of course, that the boundaries of medicine are expanding in many new directions from plastic surgery for aesthetic reasons to wellness clinics and sports medicine. But in using the concept of a "shortage of patients" in the title of the Conference, we refer to the classic domain of therapeutic medicine, not to the new extended areas. Our title therefore is a rhetorical as much as an analytic device. Our aim was to help the conferees focus on the implications of a steadily growing supply of physicians in tandem with a current and prospective decline in the demand for hospital and ambulatory care.

The authors of the five chapters were asked to deal with the following major themes:

- Changes in the pool of applicants and matriculants to U.S. medical schools with a look to probable developments between now and the end of the 1980s.
- Changes in physician practice modes in terms of solo, group, salaried, and prepaid arrangements and also changes in patient loads, work hours, incomes, and operating costs.
- The likely effects for physicians of the major changes that are under way as well as other changes that loom on the horizon. However painful some of these changes may be for individual physicians who find their expectations unfulfilled, we asked Professor Stevens to use a much wider lens and explore how past, present, and future changes are likely to alter the role of the medical profession in a better educated, richer, technologically advanced country such as the United States.
- Convinced that we would learn as much by focusing on micro developments as on macro trends, we invited Dr. Stephen C. Schoenbaum, the Deputy Director of the Harvard Community Health Plan, to outline the experience of this unusual health maintenance organization in the use of different types of health personnel.
- The other micro study was centered on a geographic area, the San Francisco Bay Area, which has been characterized by two developments critical to our agenda: a large supply of physicians and radical changes in the ways in which physicians practice.

So much for the focus of each of the five chapters that forms the heart of this volume. To achieve our second goal of helping the reader to understand the forces that lie back of the major changes under way on both supply and practice, we will review each in turn.

The first direct effort of the Congress to increase the supply of physicians occurred in 1963 after the long-term opposition of the AMA was muted because of its preoccupation with defeating Medicare. For the remainder of the decade and until 1971 Congress passed a large number of bills aimed at the same goal: to overcome the shortage in physician personnel, variously estimated at 50,000, 80,000, 100,000.

In 1971 Congress acted on its belief that physician personnel constituted a national asset since many physicians educated in one state eventually practiced in another; accordingly it could justify through "capitation" a federal contribution to the costs of undergraduate medical education.

In its enthusiasm Congress went further: it decoupled capitation assistance from any reciprocal action on the part of the medical schools, such as increased enrollments, and it provided similar capitation payments for other health professions.

Extending its reach beyond undergraduate medical education, Congress undertook to finance residency training programs in family practice in the belief that only by such action would the supply of primary care physicians adequately meet the demand for such services.

Two years later Dr. Charles Edwards, Assistant Secretary for Health, informed Congress that the Administration had concluded that the physician shortage had ended and a potential surplus loomed ahead.

In the waning days of the Ford Administration, the Secretary of HEW in 1975 appointed an advisory committee to examine the trends in physician personnel; however, it was not until after the election of President Carter that the new Secretary of HEW, Joseph Califano, reconstituted the committee and gave it a broad charter. The Graduate Medical Education National Advisory Committee (GMENAC), under the chairmanship of Dr. Alvin Tarlov, undertook the most ambitious review of physician personnel—its current status and future outlook— ever launched in the United States. The committee reported its findings in the fall of 1980, projecting a serious aggregate surplus (70,000) in 1990 and a still larger surplus (140,000) in the year 2000. It concluded that many specialties and subspecialties would be in oversupply, and that only a few fields would confront shortfalls.

Although Dr. Tarlov had relied extensively on the judgment of physicians in calculating both future requirements and future supply, the medical establishment responded either with silence or with snide or frontal attacks on his methodology; in fact, it challenged his conclusions.

In 1976, Congress amended the federal health personnel legislation and formally declared that the physician shortage had ended, but it continued to exert its influence by making future federal support to medical schools contingent upon their ensuring that at least 50 percent of their graduates would pursue primary care residencies. This legislative intervention failed as the result of strong protest from some leading schools and the belated perception that the desired ratio had already been achieved. Congress terminated all capitation payments for health professional schools in 1981, a mere ten years after it had first initiated such support.

The quinquennium since the publication of the GMENAC report can be summarized as follows: The continuing reluctance of the medical establishment to speak out clearly on the issue of physician supply, ostensibly because of the threat of anti-trust prosecution but more importantly because of the inability of the leadership to achieve a consensus and mobilize for action. The leaders of many specialty groups have been loath to take the bold step of advocating reduced recruitment to their ranks because they fear that competing specialties might not follow suit. Most directors of residency training programs believe that a loss of power and prestige would follow cutbacks in their programs. Since there is a continuing inflow into the United States of a large number of poorly trained FMGs and USFMGs, many informed persons, physicians and nonphysicians alike, believe that it makes little sense to cut back on U.S. trained physicians. And so far it has been difficult to stop the inflow. Moreover, many hospitals in some states believe that they cannot continue to perform their missions without FMGs and USFMGs.

A few medical schools, under state or private auspices, have reduced entering classes but very modestly; admissions for 1984–1985 and 1985–1986 were only slightly below those in earlier years.

However, the nature of the flow of students into medicine has been radically altered by the fact that women currently account for one-third of the entering class, up from about 10 percent at the beginning of the 1960s. Two related points: had it not been for this large new pool of exceptionally well-prepared women applicants, U.S. medical schools would have long ago faced a Hobson's choice—either to reduce their standards for admission or cut back on the size of the student body. It is not clear that the pool of highly qualified women will increase in the face of dominant demographic and economic trends, i.e., the decline in the number of the college age cohort and the negative impact of both higher medical school tuition and lower physicians' earnings.

The enlarged proportion of women in the medical profession has unquestionably led many interested parties to refrain from advocating a policy aimed at reducing the number of accepted applicants to medical school. Projecting from historical experience that women have tended to work fewer hours and fewer years than male physicians (about 20 percent less in the course of a career), they regard the increasing proportion of women physicians as a significant buffer to the threatened oversupply.

Some analysts have been reluctant to press for a reduction of student enrollments on other grounds, in particular the fear that with fewer physicians available, access of the poor to health care would prove more problematic, new forms of service delivery would be difficult to launch, and the costs of treatment would be greater.

A word about each of these last reservations: We doubt that improved access of the poor to medical care depends on the size of the total pool of physicians as much as on the organizational and financial arrangements that can facilitate outreach and thus enable the poor to enter the mainstream. That an enlarged supply of medical personnel will facilitate experimentation with new delivery forms is hard to challenge. But the assumption that a larger supply of physicians will result in lower costs is wrong. The unit cost per service will decline, but that does not apply to the total costs to the system from a much larger supply of physicians. In the 1960s and early 1970s, powerful forces were operating at both state and federal levels to increase the supply of registered nurses and allied health personnel in the belief that the shortages of physicians could be significantly ameliorated by such actions. However, the nation never reached a consensus about the use of allied health personnel as substitutes for or collaborators with physicians. GMENAC made some straddling assumptions by projecting the current level of training such personnel into the future, and advocating neither their enhanced nor reduced output.

Contradictory trends are currently at work. On the one hand, as physicians become less busy while the expenses of operating a fee-for-service practice mount, physicians are less likely to add to their support staff. Moreover, there has been a decline of 10 to 15 percent in the employment of hospital personnel since 1983, and this decline is likely to continue as cost-reimbursement pressures accelerate. On the other hand, the growth of large, managed systems of care (particularly prepaid systems) provides additional opportunities for cost savings based on the greater utilization of allied health personnel. It is difficult to foretell which of these factors will dominate in the years ahead.

As of the beginning of 1986 the following represents a summary of the outlook for physicians:

- A continued rise in the proportion of physicians per 100,000 population from 140 in 1950 to possibly double that number by the end of the century. The ratio in 1986 is over 220 per 100,000.
- There is diffuse criticism from many members of the profession who believe that the trend toward still larger numbers of physicians is contraindicated and that new enrollments in medical schools should be curtailed. There is broader agreement that the first step should be a radical reduction in the number of FMGs accepted for residency training.
- It is widely held, especially among health policy analysts, that maldistribution both by specialty and location have not been effectively addressed but no clear alternatives have been formulated.
- There is no agreement in the decision-making arenas about preferred policy with respect to the future of allied health personnel.
- There is mounting evidence that the pool of highly qualified students applying to medical schools has decreased and will probably shrink further.

- There is at least one direct relationship between trends in the number of physicians and changes in physician practices. A large annual increment of physicians entering practice makes it easier for the managers of new delivery systems to attract the numbers and types of physicians they need to experiment with innovative forms of health service delivery. The indolent growth of HMOs until the early 1980s was in part a result of the difficulties faced by prepayment plans attempting to attract physicians to practice in a mode other than fee-for-service. The marked increase in HMOs—of all varieties—since 1980 in no small measure reflects the growing availability of young physicians who, when they are ready to enter practice, are seeking alternatives to fee-for-service medicine. They do not want to add to their considerable educational indebtedness the costs of establishing a private practice.

The growth of for-profit hospital chains in the 1970s was assisted by the easing of the physician supply. Many physicians who were not firmly established were disposed to accept incentives offered by for-profit chains to relocate to communities where a newly acquired hospital was operating. Hospital chains were willing to provide a physician's office and other support services under highly favorable terms in order to broaden and deepen their attending staffs.

During the last decade, there has been a marked increase in the proportion of physicians who are engaged wholly or partly in salaried practice. Moreover, many of these "salaried" physicians are full-time employees of a corporate medical enterprise operating on a for-profit basis. This is true of a wide variety of new provider forms, from emergency medical units to surgi-centers, and walk-in clinics, and many other types.

Although Blue Cross plans had long been able to negotiate special prices with the hospitals that treated large numbers of their patients, discounts based on volume, speed of reimbursement, and other economic benefits, such discounts were the exception rather than the rule in the health care sector. Recently, the combination of excess hospital capacity and an increase in the number of physicians who are working fewer hours than they would like has stimulated the growth of PPO and similar arrangements which, in essence, result in discounts to payers for an assured volume of enrollees. The most rapid growth in HMOs has been in the IPA model, which imposes an economic risk upon participating physicians and also obliges them to treat selected patients for less than their accustomed fees.

Studies of these new forms of health care delivery have not revealed any striking differences in their use of physicians. There is evidence that HMOs are able to care for their members with a ratio of approximately 110 physicians per 100,000, about one-half of the national average. Part of the explanation is that HMOs make many fewer referrals to hospitals and rely on allied health personnel to assist their corps of physicians. Another part of the explanation is that most HMOs make little or no contribution to medical education or medical research, activities that make heavy use of physicians.

The chairman of the GMENAC Report, Dr. Tarlov, recently called attention to the fact that the rapid growth of HMOs required a recalculation of the estimated surplus of physicians in 1990 and 2000. The shrinking "fee-for-service" component of U.S. medicine, in contrast to the prepaid component, would find it more difficult to absorb increasing numbers of physicians.

When a physician has completed his or her professional training he or she has a prospective working life of thirty-five to forty years. Relatively few licensed physicians are occupationally mobile; they do not opt out of medicine for a new and different career. Therefore, one faces the question of the likely utilization of the larger numbers of physicians who are entering the profession. The following dimensions are noteworthy:

- We called attention earlier to the proposition that the much larger proportion of women physicians will absorb part of this calculated surplus because they usually have a more restricted work schedule and working life.
- Most younger male physicians are working a shorter workweek than their colleagues of the 1950s and 1960s. This trend toward a shorter workweek will probably continue.
- The boundaries of medicine are expanding into different types of "wellness programs" which will provide employment opportunities for some physicians.
- The same "boundary extensions" are taking place in selected surgical specialties.

On the other side, we must take account of such factors as:

- The growth of "protocol" medicine aimed at establishing standards that physicians must follow. A major objective of these new standards is to control "unnecessary" and costly interventions.
- A growing perception on the part of some sectors of the public (the better educated, higher income groups) that they are in a better position to protect their own health and that it is dysfunctional to "overuse" the health care system.

- The restructuring of insurance benefits to impose higher deductibles on the users of services which will tend to moderate demand.

It is difficult to foresee how these conflicting trends—more physicians, new forms of health care delivery, new financial arrangements, the expanded boundaries of medicine, more self-care—will play themselves out. The first Cornell University Medical College Conference on Health Policy (1985) highlighted serious and growing problems arising from the breakdown in payment mechanisms to provide continued access to the health care system for the uncovered population, particularly the poor.

The following paragraphs set forth some of the themes that surface in each of the five chapters.

Chapter 2: U.S. Medical School Applicants and Matriculants, 1960–1985 and Beyond

- In light of the trends in applications to medical schools, can the United States afford to follow the advice of the AMA and rely on the market to balance capacity and need or should it develop an intervention policy? And if the latter, what kind of policy?
- The trend data point to declining numbers of applicants from minorities and low-income families. Do we need a policy to counter this trend and, if so, what are the prospects for reversing the declines?
- How much sense does it make to maintain a ratio of approximately one faculty member per student in medical school? And to rely increasingly on faculty practice income to provide a major part of the funding for medical education? What steps can be taken to place medical education on a sounder financial basis?

Chapter 3: Physician Personnel and Physician Practice

- Are we moving into a period when there will be a shortage of patients? If so, what will be some of the likely consequences?
- Physicians' incomes have begun to level off or decline (in real terms) while their expenses (including malpractice insurance premiums) continue to rise. Moreover, many young graduates are entering practice with sizable and growing debts. What will be the responses to these untoward trends?

- The U.S. public has less positive views about physicians in general than it had a decade or two ago. What are the likely consequences of this attitudinal change for political action in the future?

Chapter 4: The Future of the Medical Profession

- Corporatization of medical care is advancing. More and more physicians will be working in environments where their status will be that of "employees." What are the likely consequences of this shift for physician performance and/or patient satisfaction?
- Is it really possible (consider the U.K. and other countries) to displace physicians from key decision-making roles in the operation of the health care system? If not, how does the corporatization trend balance out with the continuing dominance of the profession?
- U.S. medicine since World War II has been dominated by the trend toward specialization in which residency review committees and the specialty boards have played leading roles. What are the prospects that these important institutions will be weakened in the decades ahead and what are some of the likely consequences?

Chapter 5: Employment of Physicians at Harvard Community Health Plan

- Are the present forecasts of continuing rapid growth likely to be correct or will the expansion be more moderate? To what extent is it valid to regard the IPA model as a close variant of the staff or group model?
- Assuming moderate or high growth of HMOs, will the "surplus" of physicians, particularly specialists and subspecialists, be significantly worsened and what public policies are called for to moderate the adverse effects?
- How does the following circle get squared: the increasing supply of physicians intent on protecting their income expectations; HMOs doing their best to keep enrollees out of hospitals and controlling referrals to specialists; and hospitals seeking to maintain their inpatient census?

Chapter 6: A Lifestyle Decision:
Facing the Reality of Physician Oversupply
in the San Francisco Bay Area

- To what extent are there growing numbers of large cities such as San Francisco in which it is difficult/impossible for young physicians to start up in solo or group practices? Will the list of "closed" cities be much longer by 1990/1995?
- How many years will it be before cities with physician-to- population ratios in the 300–400 per 100,000 range have few salaried positions in hospitals/HMOs for young/older physicians? If more and more cities are "closed," where will the new graduates go?
- The San Francisco situation reveals that many established private practitioners are joining various plans, particularly PPOs, in a desperate effort to maintain a desired patient load. At what point do these multiple linkages with differing conditions of practice, fee schedules, etc. become unmanageable in the sense of excessive administrative, accounting, overhead costs? How can practice arrangements be simplified?

The foregoing questions are only suggestive of the rich materials contained in the following chapters. But they provide some initial orientation to the intriguing subject of a surplus of physicians in an era of possibly declining demand for health care.

2

U.S. Medical School Applicants and Matriculants, 1960–1985 and Beyond

August G. Swanson

The past quarter-century has been a period of extraordinary expansion in the educational, research, and service capacities of the nation's medical schools. Stimulated by predictions that there would be too few physicians to meet the medical needs of an expanding population,[1] forty-one medical schools were founded in this era, and existing schools increased their enrollment. The result was an increase in the number of graduates from 7,081 in 1960 to 16,318 in 1985.

This doubling of the number of new physicians was achieved through the interaction of several public policy decisions that facilitated the expansion of faculties, the construction of research and teaching facilities, the direct federal support of medical education, and the enlargement of the clinical facilities available for both teaching and research. Thus, the direct support of university-based biomedical research beginning in the late 1940s laid the foundation for recruiting faculty. The 1963 and subsequent health manpower acts made federal funds available for the construction of teaching facilities, initiated federal scholarship and loan support for medical students, and provided direct support for educational program development. The passage of Medicare-Medicaid legislation in 1965 not only made medical care available to a large number of elderly and needy Americans, but it also began the erosion of a two-class system of medical care. The clinical education of medical students and residents, traditionally confined to public hospitals and charity services, was extended into private hospitals. As a result, medical school clinical faculties increased to care for patients and to teach students and residents in this new environment.

These events alone might not have enlarged the graduating classes of our medical schools had there also not been a great increase in the number of young men and women who wanted to be physicians. In 1960 the ratio between applicants and those accepted to medical school fell to 1.7, the lowest in the postwar era (Figure 2.1).[2] During the 1960s this ratio slowly increased and was 2.2 by 1970. A ratio of 2.8 applicants for each position was achieved in 1973 and this ratio persisted through 1975. From 1970 to 1975, the number of available places in medical schools increased by 3,865 (25 percent), rising from 11,500 to 15,365, and the number of applicants grew 42 percent from 24,987 to a maximum of 42,624 in 1974 (Figure 2.2).

This extraordinary increase in medical school applicants was in part due to the rising number of college graduates produced by the postwar "baby boom," but there was also a heightened interest in medicine as a career in this population. In 1960 the proportion of applicants expressed as a percentage of twenty-two-year-olds in the population was only 0.64 percent. In 1974 this percentage had increased 1.8 times to 1.15 percent.[3] The motivations of these aspirants for a career in medicine are not clear. Certainly, the almost universal acceptance of the need for more physicians stimulated their interest. The apparent increasing affluence of doctors, particularly after the passage of Medicare, must have attracted many, but there also was a tide of student activism directed toward social reform that was consistent with the traditional service role of the medical profession.

The feminist movement and its effect on the career aspirations of women was the greatest contributor to the expansion of the country's medical school classes. Had the percentage of women-to-men applicants remained in the 10 percent range of the 1960s, by 1975 there would have been only 35,700 applicants for 15,365 positions, a ratio of 2.3. Instead, the number of women applicants increased 3.5 times, from 2,734 in 1970 to 9,575 in 1975 and the proportion of women in the entering class increased from 11.3 percent to 23.7 percent.

Affirmative action programs to increase the opportunities in medical education for underrepresented minority students also contributed to the enlarged pool of applicants. In 1970 there were only 1,230 black applicants; by 1975 there were 2,288. Mexican American, American Indian, and mainland Puerto Rican applicants also increased. In 1975 there were 3,049 minority applicants (Table 2.1). Of these, 1,308 were accepted and minority students comprised 10 percent of the first-year enrollment that year.

Applicants Decrease

During the decade of 1975–1985 the number of medical school applicants declined while the number of positions in the medical schools continued to increase through 1981 (Figure 2.3). In 1985 there were 32,893 applicants for 17,312 positions, or 1.9 applicants per position. The proportion of applicants expressed as a percentage of twenty-two-year-olds in the population is now 0.77 percent, which is indicative of a declining interest in medicine as a career among that age group. The greatest decrease has been among white males, who dropped from 32,515 in 1975 to 21,331 in 1985. In 1985, white males constituted only 64 percent of the applicant pool, while women accounted for 36 percent.

The rate of decrease in medical school applicants has not been uniform. Between 1977 and 1978 there was a 10 percent drop in total applicants. During the subsequent six years, the total number of applicants remained stable, but in 1985 the total number of applicants decreased by 8.5 percent. For the first time this decrease included women, who dropped 7.3 percent and underrepresented minorities, who fell 7.2 percent. The 1977–1978 drop has been attributed to the introduction of a new Medical College Admission Test (MCAT). The medical schools required applicants to the 1978 class to submit scores on the new examination, which discouraged some students from reapplying since their old MCAT scores were not recognized. The decrease in 1985, however, appears to be a change in the rate of decrease that signals a persistent change in the slope of the curve. Data for applicants to the 1986 class indicate that a similar decrease will occur next year. If a continued decline in applicants continues through 1990, the number of persons with the qualifications needed to study medicine may be insufficient to maintain an entering class approaching the present size.

In 1981 the entering class in U.S. medical schools reached a peak of 16,644, and since then has dropped at the rate of 0.6 percent per year. Table 2.2 projects the number of applicants through 1990 for a 4 percent and an 8 percent per year rate of decline, and the number of matriculants at 0.6 percent per year, 4 percent per year, and 8 percent per year rates of decrease. Table 2.3 shows the applicant/position ratio if the 0.6 percent per year decrease in matriculants should persist. With a 4 percent per year decrease, the ratio will reach its 1960 level of 1.7 by 1990. However, if the rate is 8 percent per year, the ratio will be 1.6 by 1988 and could fall to 1.4 by 1990.

In the 1950s and early 1960s when the applicant/position ratio ranged below 2, the attrition rate rose to above 10 percent. The Association of American Medical Colleges (AAMC) was sufficiently concerned about the academic qualifications of medical students that it conducted a major study entitled, "Doctor or Dropout," which was published in 1966.[4] The study found that half of the year-to-year variance in attrition rate can be accounted for by the size of the applicant pool. Should this hold true as the applicant pool declines during the next five years, the number of graduates from medical school will decrease because of both an increase in attrition from its present 1 to 2 percent level and a shrinkage in class size as medical schools reduce enrollments because of a perceived lack of qualified candidates. The author anticipates that the entering class size of 1990 will be between 13,500 and 14,000.

Thus far, the academic ability of medical school matriculants as measured by grade point averages (GPAs) and Medical College Admissions Test (MCAT) scores has not declined significantly, but since 1980 there has been a slight downward shift in GPAs (Table 2.4). In 1980, 77.4 percent of the entering class had GPAs between 3.3 and 4.0. Only 73.5 percent of the 1985 class had GPAs in this range. The proportion with GPAs in the 3.0–3.29 range increased by 3.1 percent from 1981 to 1985. MCAT scores have tended to increase. In 1980, 52.5 percent of the entering class had Science Problems scores of 10 or above. This increased to 59.5 percent of the class of 1985. This upward shift is explained by an overall increase in scores in the MCAT science subtests due to greater familiarity of candidates with the content of this portion of the examination. The distribution of the reading subtest scores has remained essentially constant.

The drop in applicants is not uniformly distributed among the states (Table 2.5). Between 1981 and 1985, the resident applicants from five states (District of Columbia, Louisiana, Minnesota, South Dakota, and Vermont) fell by 30 percent or more. Aplicants from six states (Arizona, Delaware, Georgia, Nevada, Texas, and Wyoming) increased slightly ranging from 4.2 percent to 9.1 percent. The remainder of the states all experienced decreases over this five-year period ranging from 0.3 percent in California to 25 percent in Hawaii.

The decline in applicants also increased the proportion of candidates admitted, but the increase is disproportional geographically (Tables 2.6 and 2.7). Between 1981 and 1985 the proportion of resident applicants from seven states (Minnesota, Montana, New Hampshire, New Mexico, North Carolina, Utah, and Wyoming) admitted to medical schools increased by more than 10 percent. In ten states (Idaho, Indiana, Kentucky, North Dakota, Puerto Rico, South Carolina, Tennessee, Texas, Vermont, and Washington), the percentage of residents admitted decreased from 0.7 percent to 2.6 percent.

Kansas, with 200 out of 309 (64.7 percent) of its residents admitted to medical schools in 1985, has consistently had the highest proportion of its applicants admitted since 1981. With a class size of 200, the

University of Kansas School of Medicine has had to increase the number of out-of-state residents admitted, presumably because the quality of the in-state pool is deemed insufficient. In 1981, 94.5 percent of the entering class at the University of Kansas School of Medicine were Kansas residents; in 1985 that proportion had fallen to 86.5 percent. In the aggregate, U.S. medical schools admitted 682 more out-of-state students in 1985 than in 1981 indicating a loosening of residency restrictions among the states.

Another indicator of change in the applicant pool is an increase in the number of applicants who received an acceptance from more than one medical school (Table 2.8). In 1981, 38.4 percent of those accepted received acceptances from two or more schools. In 1985, 41.6 percent received two or more acceptances. It is expected that this competition for a restricted number of qualified candidates will intensify as the number of medical school applicants falls.

There are other qualitative changes in medical school applicants. Through a questionnaire filled out by applicants when they take the MCAT, the following changes in applicants' characteristics between 1980 and 1985 were discerned.

There is a shift toward applicants coming from more affluent social strata. In 1980, 36.3 percent of applicants' fathers were physicians or other professionals. This proportion increased to 39 percent in 1985. In 1980, 22.8 percent of applicants' fathers had doctoral degrees, compared to 25.9 percent in 1985. The proportion whose fathers had not completed high school fell from 10.7 percent to 8.7 percent.

Those from families with incomes of $30,000 a year or more increased from 40.8 percent to 53.8 percent, and those from families with incomes in the $5,000 to $10,000 a year range dropped from 6.4 percent to 3.7 percent. Despite this upward shift in family incomes, the 1985 applicants were more indebted than those in 1980 when 63.7 percent had no educational debts and only 2.6 percent had debts of $10,000 or more. In 1985, 47.4 percent had no debt and 10.6 percent had debts of $10,000 or greater.

There has also been a shift in the location of where applicants attended high school. In 1980, 32.4 percent had gone to high school in the suburbs of large or medium-sized cities and 8.5 percent had attended small-town or rural high schools. In 1985, these proportions had shifted to 33.7 percent in the suburbs and 7.4 percent in small towns or rural areas.

Consistent with this shift toward urban and away from rural origins is the change in applicants' hopes for locating their practices. In 1980, 18.2 percent of the applicants planned to practice in towns of 10,000 or less and in rural areas. Only 10.4 percent of the 1985 applicants expressed such plans. A commensurate increase is seen in the proportion planning to practice in large cities or their suburbs. In 1980, 23.4 percent planned to locate in large cities or their suburbs. This increased to 30 percent for 1985 applicants.

Although applicants to medical school must be considered relatively naive and unsophisticated about the careers they might ultimately choose in medicine, there have been striking changes in applicants' plans for specialties. In 1980, 38.9 percent indicated they planned to be family or general practitioners, and 18.1 percent hoped to be surgeons. In 1985, only 23.2 percent planned a family or general practice and the proportion planning to specialize in surgery increased to 27.6 percent. Of the 1980 applicants, 34 percent expected to be in private practice, and 18.3 percent expected to be employed by a hospital or other organization. In 1985 these proportions had changed to 30 percent expecting private practice, and 21.9 percent expecting to be employed.

It is of interest that similar shifts in career expectations are seen among medical school graduates (Table 2.9). The responses to the AAMC Graduation Questionnaire of the class of 1982 and of the class of 1985 indicate a distinct shift away from the primary care specialties, ranging from a 12.6 percent decrease in family practice to a 25.9 percent decrease in general internal medicine. The largest increases are in anesthesiology, emergency medicine, diagnostic radiology, and the medical and pediatric subspecialties. General surgery and the surgical subspecialties are relatively unchanged. This may be due to students' perceptions that residency positions in those specialties are highly competitive, while the hospital-based specialties are less competitive. An alternative explanation is that anesthesiology, emergency medicine, and radiology will provide more secure employment opportunities for physicians who have completed their training. The fact that the average debt of 1985 graduates planning to be certified in emergency medicine was $3,500 higher than the $30,000 average for all seniors suggests that a shorter training program and the prospect of immediate employment thereafter makes this specialty attractive for students with high debts. Another trend consistent with the movement away from primary care toward more remunerative specialties is a change in the proportion of graduates who plan to practice in a small city, town, or rural area. In 1982, 24.9 percent of the graduating class indicated that these were their preferred locations. This dropped to 19.2 percent for the class of 1985. Fewer members of the class of 1985 expect to be in private practice. Only 57.9 percent indicated they plan such careers compared to 64.4 percent of the 1982 graduates.

The increasing indebtedness of medical school graduates is of concern and may account for both the shift away from primary care specialties and the trend toward locating in larger metropolitan areas. Between

1981 and 1985 the average debt of graduating seniors increased by 34.2 percent from $19,697 to $29,943 (Table 2.10). The number of graduates who had debts of $40,000 or more increased from 248 in 1981 to 2,356 in 1982 (Figure 2.4). Those with high educational debt have borrowed considerable amounts through market-rate interest loan programs, such as Auxiliary Loans to Assist Students (ALAS) and Health Education Assistance Loans (HEAL). These high interest loans without interest subsidies while students are in school place burdensome payback obligations on new physicians, either during or immediately upon completion of their graduate medical education. If both employment or private practice opportunities for physicians entering the profession become limited and those with significant debt are forced to default or declare bankruptcy, this negative financial experience may further decrease the interest of college students in careers in medicine.

The Faculties

The slow decline in the number of entering medical students since 1981 has not been accompanied by a reduction in faculty size. Indeed, while the entering class has decreased at the rate of 0.6 percent per year since 1981, the total faculty size has increased at the rate of 2.8 percent per year from 50,532 to 58,779 (Table 2.11). This 8,247 expansion in faculty size provides a student/faculty ratio of 1.1. In 1960, when the total faculty in U.S. medical schools numbered only 11,224, the ratio was 2.7.

These data illustrate the dramatic change in the nature of medical schools, which have undergone a metamorphosis from a collection of relatively small institutions engaged principally in research and medical education into academic medical centers with an enlargement of their educational programs to include large numbers of residents and fellows and an expansion of their clinical services. Research programs have also grown, but the basic science faculties, whose growth has been driven by research funding, increased only threefold from 1960 to 1984, while the clinical faculties have increased sixfold. In the five years between 1981 and 1984, basic science faculties increased by 4.1 percent, while clinical departments grew 10.8 percent.

This increase in full-time medical school faculties has had little to do with the increase in medical student enrollments. In fact, as faculties have grown to accomplish institutional research and service commitments, the medical student educational program has suffered from too many faculty members spending too little time with medical students. A frequent complaint to the Panel on the General Professional Education of the Physician[5] was that both faculty members and students had little opportunity to get to know each other because faculties divide their time commitments to the medical student program among too many people.

The sources of revenue for the general operating support of medical schools are changing; there is greater reliance on faculty practice income and less on sponsored research and state support (Table 2.12). Income from the provision of medical services by the faculties increased from $1,850 million in 1980 to $2,980 million in 1983, an increase of 37.9 percent and a shift from practice income providing 47.5 percent of general operating revenues of the schools to practice income providing 51.8 percent. Although federal research support and state and local government contributions increased over this four-year period, the increase was only 20.6 percent and 23.4 percent respectively.

It can be assumed that a reduction in medical school class size will have only a marginal effect on faculty size. State appropriations for medical students are generally based on a full-time equivalent faculty/ student ratio, and some states will reduce their contributions, but the revenues from clinical services have thus far offset these losses. Similarly for private schools, lower tuition revenues may be made up by medical practice income. Research support is unlikely to sustain faculties except in a few prestigious, research-intensive institutions.

There are in process changes in research support, the organization of the medical care system, and payment policies for medical services that could rapidly alter the size of medical school faculties. The federal government's resolve to control the deficit by reducing domestic expenditures eventually will decrease institutional research programs. This will principally affect basic scientists who have increasingly had to use research grants for salary support. The increased competition among providers of medical care for patients could result in the expansion or contraction of medical school faculties. Some schools may bring in more clinicians to increase their service programs and practice revenues. Others may have to contract and limit their clinical services to patients with complex problems requiring tertiary care.

The Future

Hazardous as making predictions may be, it is important that those responsible for the education of physicians and the stewardship of academic medicine plans to accommodate foreseeable changes over which they have only marginal control. Although medical education in the United States has an illustrious record, it can be improved. It must be adapted to a reorganization of the medical care system and to a retreat from the support of biomedical research and social programs by both the executive branch and the Congress. Those responsible for leadership in our academic medical centers were educated and assumed their careers in a period of growth and expansion. Continuing imaginative leadership during a period of downsizing and consolidation imposes a different set of challenges.

Competing for Students

The rising costs of medical education for students, as reflected in their indebtedness on graduation, and opportunities for alternative careers that require shorter, less arduous preparation, will challenge medical school deans and their faculties to make the study of medicine an intellectually stimulating and personally fulfilling experience. For the foreseeable future, the number of qualified applicants will steadily decrease. Those who do matriculate will have to pay for their education, and the prospects for assured high incomes when their education is completed will dim. Those schools that become student-focused and modify their educational programs in the directions recommended by the Panel on the General Professional Education of the Physician (GPEP) are more likely to attract the best students.

Thus far, the GPEP Report has stimulated considerable discussion among faculties but, to date, there is little measurable outcome. The amorphous decision-making process for the medical student curriculum in most institutions makes major changes from traditional approaches very difficult to achieve. Faculties and disciplinary departments have authority over curriculum; deans have the responsibility for its administration. This separation of authority from responsibility was of prime concern to the GPEP Panel, which recommended that medical school deans should identify and designate an interdisciplinary and interdepartmental organization of faculty members to formulate a coherent and comprehensive educational program for medical students and to select the instructional and evaluative methods to be used. The Panel recommended that this group have the responsibility and the authority to plan, implement, and supervise an integrated program of general professional education. This recommendation has been widely discussed, but its implementation is in abeyance in almost all institutions.

The two major changes recommended by the GPEP Panel that are the most challenging are: (1) Moving from an information-intensive mode of education, in which faculties assume that their task is to tell students what they know about their narrow area of research or specialization, to a mode of guiding students in independent learning; (2) Creating an environment for clinical education that will provide the opportunity for medical students to acquire the basic clinical knowledge and skills, and the values and attitudes that all physicians must have.

Independent Learning

Several schools (Harvard, New Mexico, Southern Illinois University, and McMaster University, Canada) have introduced problem-based teaching and learning that require students to seek the information they need to solve problems posed by their teachers. This educational technique is difficult to adopt and is time-consuming. Faculty members who commit themselves to these programs have less time for research. Since competition for research funding is increasing, it is difficult to find the resources to support those who are both capable and willing to be involved with medical student education. Except for a few schools, outside funding is not likely to be available in significant amounts. Rebudgeting of existing resources will be required.

Clinical Education

Traditional teaching hospitals, owned by or closely affiliated with medical schools, have become increasingly complex institutions providing highly specialized tertiary care. In addition, reductions in length of stay and the trend toward having much of patients' diagnostic workups accomplished prior to hospitalization reduce the opportunities for medical students to work up and study patients with common problems. At a conference on the clinical education of medical students sponsored by the AAMC in September 1985, there was a consensus among participants that ambulatory care settings must be used for medical students' clinical education. However, most schools have only limited ambulatory care facilities that are satisfactory for educating students. The reduction in productivity that results when students are incorporated into outpatient clinics is a significant deterrent. For example, health maintenance organizations are reluctant to permit students to be involved in their clinics unless payment is received from the school to offset their costs. Since medical schools rarely budget the direct costs of medical students' clinical education, the wide use of ambulatory clinics as a partial substitute for teaching hospital services will also require shifting financial priorities.

Graduate Medical Education

Finally, if medical school classes decrease in size, there ultimately will be fewer graduates seeking residency training. In the 1960s and 1970s, the shortfall in U.S. graduates was balanced by a large number of foreign medical graduates. Now, there is a national thrust toward limiting the entry of foreign medical graduates into accredited graduate medical education programs. The combination of a reduced domestic output and limited foreign entry will mean that by the 1990s the number of graduate medical education positions available may far exceed the need. For example, there were over 7,000 entry-level positions available in internal medicine in 1985. If the number of first-year students decreases at a rate of between 4 percent to 8 percent between 1986 and 1990, by 1994 the number of internal medicine positions needed by domestic graduates will be between 3,500 and 4,300. Accommodating this reduction has serious implications for both the service obligations of teaching hospitals and the quality of graduate medical education.

Summary

After a period of unprecedented expansion in medical education that more than doubled the annual output of physicians, the medical schools now face a decreasing applicant pool. At the same time federal support of biomedical research is decreasing, state support for educational programs is at a plateau and may decrease, and medical schools are increasingly dependent upon revenues from faculty practices.

Applicants and matriculants are increasing from more affluent social strata and large urban environments. They are more indebted and less interested in careers as primary care physicians.

It is expected that during the next five years a steadily shrinking pool of academically qualified applicants will increase the competition for students among the schools, some of which may modify their programs to attract good students. Ultimately, the national class size will drop to between 13,500 and 14,000. This reduction, coupled with limitations on the entry of foreign medical graduates, will result in a decreased demand for graduate medical education by the mid-1990s.

Notes

1. Dean F. Smiley, "Our Need for Doctors," *Journal of the Association of American Medical Colleges* 244 (1949): 248–250; and The Surgeon General's Consultant Group on Medical Education, "Physicians for a Growing America" (Washington, D.C.: U.S. Government Printing Office, Public Health Service Publication No. 709, 1959).

2. Davis G. Johnson, *Physicians in the Making* (San Francisco: Jossey-Bass, 1983).

3. Johnson, *Physicians in the Making.*

4. Davis G. Johnson and Edward B. Hutchins, "Doctor or Dropout?: A Study of Medical Student Attrition," *Journal of Medical Education* 41 (1966): 1097–1269.

5. Association of American Medical Colleges, "Physicians for the Twenty-First Century," *Journal of Medical Education* 59 (November 1984), Part 2.

FIGURE 2.1
Applicant/Position Ratio: U.S. Medical Schools, 1960–1985

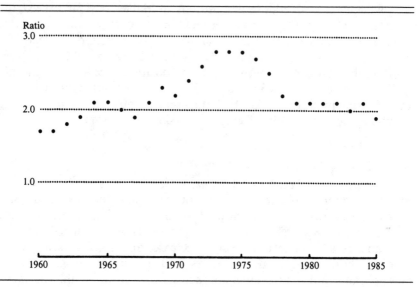

Source: Association of American Medical Colleges (AAMC) Division of Student Services.

FIGURE 2.2
Medical School Applicants, 1960–1985

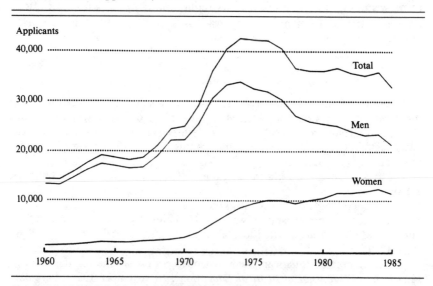

Source: AAMC Division of Student Services.

FIGURE 2.3
Accepted Applicants, 1960–1985

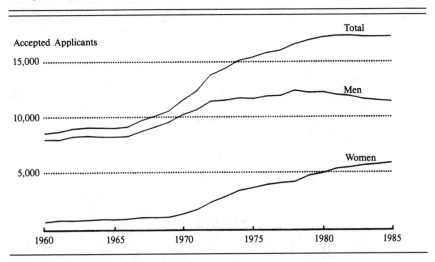

Source: AAMC Division of Student Services.

FIGURE 2.4
Indebtedness of Medical Graduates, 1981–1985

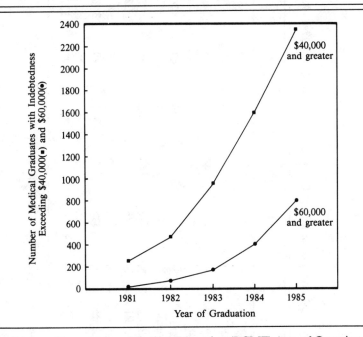

Source: Liaison Committee on Medical Education (LCME) Annual Questionnaire; AAMC.

TABLE 2.1
Accepted Minority Applicants, Percentage and Number, 1974–1984

		1974	1975	1976	1977	1978	1979	1980	1981	1982	1983	1984
Black American	%	43	41	38	39	38	39	41	39	39	40	40
	N	1,049	945	966	966	970	1,024	1,057	1,037	1,001	1,019	1,049
American Indian	%	48	43	30	35	41	42	42	43	41	43	48
	N	64	57	39	43	55	64	62	68	56	70	72
Mexican American	%	49	52	48	47	56	58	53	55	56	52	52
	N	217	220	223	227	241	267	240	281	284	263	286
Mainland Puerto Rican	%	43	43	40	46	48	53	53	51	52	55	50
	N	76	86	85	93	92	92	102	113	110	117	126
All Underrepresented	%	44	43	40	40	41	43	43	42	42	43	43
	N	1,046	1,038	1,313	1,329	1,358	1,446	1,461	1,499	1,451	1,469	1,533
All Acceptees	%	35	36	37	39	45	47	47	47	48	49	48
	N	15,066	15,365	15,774	15,977	16,527	16,886	17,146	17,286	17,294	17,209	17,194

Source: AAMC, "Minority Students in Medical Education."

TABLE 2.2
Projections of Medical School Applicants and Matriculants, 1986–1990

Decrease per year	Actual 1985	1986	1987	1988	1989	1990
APPLICANTS:	32,893					
4%		31,577	30,313	29,100	27,936	26,818
8%		30,621	27,840	25,612	23,563	21,677
MATRICULANTS:	16,282					
0.6%		16,184	16,086	15,989	15,893	15,797
4%		15,630	15,004	14,403	13,826	13,272
8%		14,979	13,780	12,677	11,662	10,729

Source: AAMC Division of Student Services.

TABLE 2.3
Projections for Applicant/Matriculant Ratio with Matriculants Decreasing by 0.6 Percent per Year, 1986–1990

	Applicant Decrease	
	4 Percent/Year	8 Percent/Year
1985 (actual)	1.90	1.90
1986	1.95	1.89
1987	1.88	1.73
1988	1.82	1.60
1989	1.76	1.48
1990	1.70	1.37

Source: AAMC Division of Student Services.

TABLE 2.4

Percentage Distribution of Grade Point Averages and Medical College Admission
Test Scores of Accepted Applicants, Selected Years, 1980–1985

Year	N	GPAs:					
		0.00–1.99	2.00–2.29	2.3–2.99	3.00–3.29	3.3–3.99	4.00
1980	15,782	<0.1	0.4	7.6	14.6	75.2	2.2
1981	16,054	<0.1	0.4	7.8	14.6	75.0	2.2
1983	15,475	<0.1	0.3	9.3	13.5	74.2	1.6
1984	15,543	<0.1	0.3	8.1	16.8	73.1	1.8
1985	15,579	<0.1	0.4	8.3	17.7	71.9	1.6

Year	N	MCAT Science Problems Scores:								
		1–4	5	6	7	8	9	10	11	12–15
1980	15,782	0.6	1.5	4.0	7.0	14.6	19.7	22.1	17.0	13.4
1981	16,054	0.7	1.8	4.3	8.1	12.4	17.7	22.1	15.4	17.4
1983	15,475	0.4	1.6	3.5	7.1	12.3	16.1	19.9	16.0	22.5
1984	15,543	0.4	1.5	3.8	7.5	11.0	15.2	22.6	15.1	22.8
1985	15,579	0.3	1.3	3.4	6.8	11.2	17.4	22.2	16.0	21.3

Source: AAMC, Medical School Admission Requirements.

TABLE 2.5
Changes in the Applicant Pool by State of Legal Residence, 1981–1984, 1984–1985, 1981–1985

State	1981 Applicants	1984 Applicants	% Change 1981–1984	1985 Applicants	% Change 1984–1985	% Change 1981–1985
Alabama	550	516	− 6.2	467	− 9.5	−15.1
Alaska	52	61	17.3	52	−14.8	0.
Arizona	340	350	2.9	362	3.4	6.5
Arkansas	356	378	6.2	322	−14.8	− 9.6
California	3,459	3,744	8.2	3,450	− 7.9	− 0.3
Colorado	533	538	0.9	459	−14.7	−13.9
Connecticut	503	461	− 8.3	420	− 8.9	−16.5
Delaware	62	74	19.4	68	8.1	9.7
District of Columbia	173	123	−28.9	116	5.7	−32.9
Florida	1,213	1,105	− 8.9	1,065	3.6	−12.2
Georgia	705	798	13.2	641	−19.7	9.1
Hawaii	220	205	− 6.8	165	−19.5	−25.0
Idaho	83	64	−22.9	74	15.6	−10.8
Illinois	1,892	1,729	− 8.6	1,660	− 4.0	−12.3
Indiana	590	675	14.4	586	−13.2	0.7
Iowa	370	346	− 6.5	327	− 5.5	−11.6
Kansas	403	334	−17.1	309	− 7.5	−23.3
Kentucky	533	515	− 3.4	473	− 8.2	−11.3
Louisiana	745	684	− 8.2	679	− 0.7	− 8.9
Maine	80	71	−11.2	52	−26.8	−35.0
Maryland	878	873	− 0.6	836	− 4.2	− 4.8
Massachusetts	1,015	1,027	1.2	975	− 5.1	− 3.9
Michigan	1,599	1,371	−14.3	1,322	− 3.6	−17.3
Minnesota	857	730	−14.8	574	−21.4	−33.0
Mississippi	381	338	−11.3	309	− 8.6	−18.9
Missouri	572	600	4.9	508	−15.3	−11.2
Montana	94	80	−14.9	72	−10.0	−23.4
Nebraska	386	373	− 3.4	320	−14.2	−17.1

continued

28

TABLE 2.5 continued

State	1981 Applicants	% Change 1981–1984	1984 Applicants	1985 Applicants	% Change 1984–1985	% Change 1981–1985
Nevada	120	11.7	134	125	− 6.7	4.2
New Hampshire	61	18.0	72	57	−20.8	− 6.6
New Jersey	1,329	− 6.0	1,249	1,167	− 6.6	−12.2
New Mexico	244	−15.6	206	195	− 5.3	−20.1
New York	3,901	− 5.0	3,704	3,413	− 7.9	−12.5
North Carolina	787	−11.1	700	642	− 8.3	−18.4
North Dakota	146	− 4.8	139	123	−11.5	−15.8
Ohio	1,605	5.7	1,697	1,554	− 8.4	− 3.2
Oklahoma	455	−13.0	396	349	−11.9	−23.3
Oregon	298	17.4	350	254	−27.4	−14.8
Pennsylvania	1,990	− 7.4	1,843	1,642	−10.9	−17.5
Puerto Rico	580	5.9	614	567	− 7.7	− 2.2
Rhode Island	117	0.9	116	112	− 3.4	− 4.3
South Carolina	412	3.6	427	396	− 7.3	− 3.9
South Dakota	149	−21.5	117	104	−11.1	−30.2
Tennessee	656	5.0	623	595	− 5.5	− 9.3
Texas	1,913	11.8	2,138	2,018	− 5.6	5.5
Utah	280	− 0.4	279	276	− 1.1	− 1.4
Vermont	98	−15.3	83	66	−10.0	−32.7
Virginia	956	−12.8	834	732	−12.2	−23.4
Washington	502	− 3.6	484	460	− 5.0	− 8.4
West Virginia	259	15.1	298	236	−20.8	− 8.9
Wisconsin	675	−14.4	578	545	− 5.7	−19.3
Wyoming	44	22.7	54	48	−11.1	9.1
**Foreign/unknown	506	27.7	646	590	8.7	16.6
Totals:	36,727	− 2.1	35,944	32,893	− 8.5	−10.4

Source: AAMC Division of Student Services.

TABLE 2.6
Applicants and Matriculants by State of Legal Residence, Number and Percentage Matriculating, 1981

State	Number of Applicants	In State	%	Out-of-State	%	Total	%
Alabama	550	207	37.6	31	5.6	238	43.3
Alaska	52	10*	19.2	10	19.2	20	38.5
Arizona	340	86	25.2	41	12.1	127	37.3
Arkansas	356	135	37.9	18	5.1	153	43.0
California	3,459	792	22.9	675	19.5	1,467	42.4
Colorado	533	118	22.1	75	14.1	193	36.2
Connecticut	503	77	15.3	120	23.9	197	39.2
Delaware	62	0	0.0	32	51.6	32	51.6
District of Columbia	173	35	20.2	21	12.1	56	32.4
Florida	1,213	327	27.0	130	10.7	457	37.7
Georgia	705	256	36.3	55	7.8	311	44.1
Hawaii	220	21	9.5	58	26.4	79	35.9
Idaho	83	20*	24.1	21	25.3	41	49.4
Illinois	1,892	762	40.3	139	7.3	901	47.6
Indiana	590	291	49.3	35	5.9	326	55.2
Iowa	370	141	38.1	12	3.2	153	41.3
Kansas	403	193	47.9	43	10.7	236	58.6
Kentucky	533	232	43.5	20	3.8	252	47.3
Louisiana	745	326	43.8	29	3.9	355	47.7
Maine	80	0	0.0	36	45.0	36	45.0
Maryland	878	185	21.1	173	19.7	358	40.8
Massachusetts	1,015	238	23.4	184	18.1	422	41.6
Michigan	1,599	543	34.0	132	8.3	675	42.2
Minnesota	857	313	36.5	59	6.9	372	43.4
Mississippi	381	149	39.1	20	5.2	169	44.3
Missouri	572	256	44.7	51	8.9	307	53.6
Montana	94	20*	21.3	23	24.5	43	45.7
Nebraska	386	163	42.2	12	3.1	175	45.3
Nevada	120	39	32.5	11	9.2	50	41.7

continued

TABLE 2.6 continued

State	Number of Applicants	In State	%	Out-of-State	%	Total	%
New Hampshire	61	15	24.6	14	22.9	29	47.5
New Jersey	1,329	278	21.0	324	24.4	602	45.4
New Mexico	244	69	28.3	16	6.6	85	34.8
New York	3,901	1,323	34.0	600	15.4	1,923	49.3
North Carolina	787	289	36.7	30	3.8	319	40.5
North Dakota	146	61	41.8	7	4.8	68	46.6
Ohio	1,605	801	49.9	78	4.9	879	54.8
Oklahoma	455	165	36.3	13	2.9	178	39.1
Oregon	298	114	38.3	35	11.7	149	50.0
Pennsylvania	1,990	773	38.8	153	7.7	926	46.5
Puerto Rico	580	261	45.0	14	2.4	275	47.4
Rhode Island	117	16	13.7	40	34.2	56	47.9
South Carolina	412	204	49.5	18	4.4	222	53.9
South Dakota	149	63	42.3	17	11.4	80	53.7
Tennessee	656	275	41.9	46	7.0	321	48.9
Texas	1,913	964	50.4	66	3.5	1,030	53.8
Utah	280	78	27.9	24	8.6	102	36.4
Vermont	98	39	39.8	7	7.1	46	46.9
Virginia	956	332	34.7	85	8.9	417	43.6
Washington	502	115	23.0	97	19.3	212	42.2
West Virginia	259	114	44.0	10	3.9	124	47.9
Wisconsin	675	273	40.4	48	7.1	321	47.5
Wyoming	44	0	0.0	24	54.5	24	54.5
**Foreign/unknown	506	N/A	N/A	71	14.0	71	14.0
Totals:	36,727	12,547	34.2	4,113	11.2	16,660	45.4

Notes: *University of Washington Medical School program.
**Includes U.S. Possessions and Canada.

Source: AAMC Division of Student Services, "Final Admission Action Summary Reports and Geographic Source of Entering Students."

TABLE 2.7
Applicants and Matriculants by State of Legal Residence, Number and Percentage Matriculating, 1985

State	Number of Applicants	In State	%	Out-of-State	%	Total	%
Alabama	467	207	44.3	28	6.0	235	50.3
Alaska	52	10*	19.2	12	23.1	22	42.3
Arizona	326	85	26.1	51	15.6	136	41.7
Arkansas	322	137	42.5	12	3.7	149	46.3
California	3,450	793	23.0	831	24.1	1,624	47.1
Colorado	459	129	28.1	69	15.0	198	43.1
Connecticut	420	93	22.1	107	25.5	200	47.6
Delaware	68	0	0.0	40	58.8	40	58.8
District of Columbia	116	27	23.3	11	9.5	38	32.8
Florida	1,065	330	31.0	152	14.3	482	45.3
Georgia	641	270	42.1	49	7.6	319	49.8
Hawaii	165	52	31.5	23	13.9	75	45.5
Idaho	74	20*	27.0	16	21.6	36	48.6
Illinois	1,660	748	45.1	133	8.01	881	53.1
Indiana	586	266	45.4	46	7.8	312	53.2
Iowa	327	144	44.0	22	6.7	166	50.8
Kansas	309	173	56.0	27	8.7	200	64.7
Kentucky	473	194	41.0	24	5.1	218	46.1
Louisiana	679	320	47.1	21	3.1	341	50.2
Maine	52	0	0.0	31	59.6	31	59.6
Maryland	836	153	18.3	232	27.8	385	46.1
Massachusetts	975	249	25.5	193	19.8	442	45.3
Michigan	1,322	474	35.9	90	6.8	564	42.7
Minnesota	574	263	45.8	44	7.6	307	53.5
Mississippi	309	110	35.6	40	12.9	150	48.5
Missouri	508	230	45.3	56	11.0	286	56.3
Montana	72	20*	27.8	21	29.2	41	56.9
Nebraska	320	128	40.0	26	8.1	154	48.1
Nevada	125	42	33.6	16	12.8	58	46.4

continued

TABLE 2.7 continued

State	Number of Applicants	In State	%	Out-of-State	%	Total	%
New Hampshire	57	7	12.3	26	45.6	33	57.9
New Jersey	1,167	281	24.1	313	26.8	594	50.9
New Mexico	195	71	36.4	22	11.3	93	47.7
New York	3,413	1,262	37.0	608	17.8	1,870	54.8
North Carolina	642	307	47.8	24	3.7	331	51.6
North Dakota	123	49	39.8	7	5.7	56	45.5
Ohio	1,554	765	49.2	106	6.8	871	56.0
Oklahoma	349	117	33.5	22	6.3	139	39.8
Oregon	254	91	35.8	36	14.2	127	50.0
Pennsylvania	1,642	679	41.4	182	11.1	861	52.4
Puerto Rico	567	245	43.2	10	1.8	255	45.0
Rhode Island	112	26	23.2	37	33.0	63	56.3
South Carolina	396	180	45.5	26	6.6	206	52.0
South Dakota	104	47	45.2	10	9.6	57	54.8
Tennessee	595	234	39.3	37	6.3	271	46.3
Texas	2,018	987	48.9	56	2.8	1,043	51.7
Utah	576	81	29.3	54	19.6	135	48.9
Vermont	66	25	37.9	4	6.1	29	43.9
Virginia	732	309	42.2	76	10.4	385	52.6
Washington	460	114	24.8	77	16.7	191	41.5
West Virginia	236	124	52.5	11	4.7	135	57.2
Wisconsin	545	253	46.4	45	8.3	298	54.7
Wyoming	48	0	0.0	33	68.8	33	68.8
**Foreign/unknown	590	N/A	N/A	120	21.6	120	20.3
Totals:	32,893	11,865	36.1	4,421	13.4	16,268	49.5

Notes: *University of Washington Medical School program.
**Includes U.S. Possessions and Canada.

Source: AAMC Division of Student Services, "Final Admission Action Summary Reports and Geographic Source of Entering Students."

TABLE 2.8
Number of Acceptances Received by Applicants, 1981, 1985

Acceptances	1981 Number	1981 Percent	1985 Number	1985 Percent
0	19,441		15,848	
1	10,652	61.6	10,056	58.4
2	3,491	20.2	3,584	20.8
3	1,565	9.1	1,731	10.0
4	734	4.2	930	5.4
5	407	2.4	463	2.7
6	189	1.1	233	1.4
7	116	0.7	118	0.7
8	63	0.4	59	0.3
9	35	0.2	25	0.1
10	18	0.1	15	0.1
11 or more	16	0.1	14	0.1
Total accepted	17,286	100.0	17,228	100.0

Source: AAMC Division of Student Services.

TABLE 2.9
Certification Plans in Selected Specialties of 1982 Graduates Compared to 1985 Graduates

Specialty	Percentage of Graduates 1982 (N = 10,938)	1985 (N = 11,047)	Percent Change
Anesthesiology	5.0%	6.6%	24.3%
Emergency medicine	2.4	3.0	20.0
Family practice	18.2	15.9	(12.6)*
General internal medicine	13.9	10.3	(25.9)
Obstetrics/gynecology	7.4	6.0	(18.9)
General pediatrics	6.8	5.6	(17.7)
Diagnostic radiology	4.5	5.4	19.7
General surgery	6.0	6.1	1.6
Orthopedic surgery	6.9	6.6	(4.4)
Otolaryngology	2.5	2.6	3.9
Ophthalmology	3.9	4.0	2.5
Medical subspecialties	3.2	4.6	30.4
Pediatric subspecialty	0.7	1.0	30.0

Note: *Decrease.

Source: AAMC Graduation Questionnaire.

TABLE 2.10
Average Debt of Indebted Medical School Graduates, 1981–1985

	Average Debt	Percent of Graduates with Debt
1981	$19,697	77%
1982	21,051	83
1983	23,647	86
1984	26,496	88
1985	29,943	87

Source: AAMC Graduation Questionnaire.

TABLE 2.11
Number of Full-time Medical School Faculty Members, 1980–1984

	1980	1981	1982	1983	1984
Basic science departments	12,816	13,223	13,587	13,488	13,783
Clinical departments	37,716	40,148	41,261	43,023	44,996
Total	50,532	53,371	54,848	56,511	58,779
Number of schools	125	126	127	127	127

Source: LCME Annual Questionnaire, Part II, AAMC.

TABLE 2.12
Financial Support of U.S. Medical Schools, 1980–1983

Revenue Source	(Dollars in Millions)				Percent Change 1980–1983
	1980	1981	1982	1983	
Federal research	$1,446	$1,578	$1,655	$1,820	20.6%
Other federal	396	415	415	390	(1.5)
State, local governments	1,452	1,617	1,784	1,896	23.4
Tuition, fees	346	413	482	545	36.5
Medical services	1,850	2,140	2,626	2,980	37.9
Other	935	1,054	1,216	1,378	32.2
Subtotal	$6,425	$7,217	$8,179	$9,010	28.7%
Less restricted revenues	−2,534	−2,749	−2,996	−3,254	22.1
Total general operating revenues	$3,891	$4,468	$5,183	$5,756	32.4%

Source: LCME Questionnaire, Part II, AAMC.

3

Physician Personnel and Physician Practice

M. Roy Schwarz

To understand the issue of physician personnel and physician practice, one must have some appreciation of the environment in which medicine is practiced. Therefore, this chapter opens with a brief overview of the environment including the economy, the demand for medical services, the accessibility of services, and future trends. This is followed by a discussion of public attitudes as they relate to physicians. An analysis of the medical profession, their numbers, practice patterns, and economics is presented next. The chapter concludes with a discussion of the market forces which are affecting physicians and physician practices.

The Environment of Medicine[1]

The U.S. Economy

Following a decade of sluggish growth and the most severe economic downturn since the Great Depression, the U.S. economy rebounded in the mid-1980s with the strongest recovery in terms of real GNP growth since the Korean War. Since 1983, the economy has been growing rapidly and it appears that a sustainable recovery is underway. Unlike previous business cycles, however, the concomitant federal budget deficit has persisted despite the impressive economic growth of the past two years. The federal budget deficit increased to $178.6 billion in calendar year 1983 from $127.9 billion in 1982. By 1985, it had reached $212.3 billion and predictions for 1986 focused on $220 billion. Correspondingly, the national debt has grown to more than $2 trillion, with 20 percent of the presidential budget request used for debt service. Fifty percent of all personal income tax receipts are used to pay the interest on the national debt.

The possibility that the economy may experience external shocks, such as the energy crisis of the 1970s, makes predicting reliable economic forecasts difficult. However, some factors suggest that the period of 1986–1999 could be one of sustained economic growth. For example, the changing demographic characteristics of the U.S. labor force are likely to provide an impetus for economic growth. Projected trends between now and the end of the century include: (1) the percentage of the labor force in the thirty-five to fifty-four age group will grow rapidly; (2) the size of the labor force will continue to increase but at a slower rate than in the recent past; and (3) the labor force participation rate of women will continue to increase.

Since workers in the thirty-five to fifty-four age group tend to be highly productive, the changing age composition of the labor force should improve the level of labor productivity. Slower overall growth in the labor force will ease pressures on business and government to create additional jobs. In addition, the increasing number of women in the labor force will tend to increase GNP.

The health sector has become an increasingly important part of the general economy. National health expenditures accounted for about 4.4 percent of GNP in 1950 and by 1982 equaled more than 10 percent of GNP. Between 1971 and 1982, health expenditures increased from $83.3 billion to $322.4 billion, an average annual increase of 13.1 percent. Between 1980 and 1983, the number of individuals employed in health services increased from 5.3 million to 6.0 million. Consequently, economic trends in the health sector can have important effects on the overall level of economic activity.

Recent projections,[2] based on the assumptions that economy-wide inflation will continue to moderate and real GNP will continue to grow, suggest that: (1) health expenditures will increase from $322.4 billion in 1982 to $690.4 billion in 1990; (2) health expenditures will account for 12.3 percent of GNP in 1990; (3) the percentage of health expenditures financed by government will remain at about 43 percent; and (4) physicians' services will continue to constitute about 21 percent of personal health care expenditures.

These projections indicate that the health sector is likely to become an even larger part of the general economy and, consequently, the influence of the health sector on the general economy will continue to grow.

Demand for Medical Services

Research has found that the level of demand for medical services and resources is related to a number of factors including: medical technology, the economy, demographic characteristics of the population, characteristics of health insurance, and accessibility of medical services.

Medical technology plays a key role in translating the patient's desire for improved health status into demand for medical resources. For example, individuals with diabetes have always desired improved health. However, until insulin was developed, that desire often was not translated into demand for medical services and resources. Conversely, advances in medical technology can reduce the demand for medical resources. For example, the development of new drugs to treat tuberculosis vastly reduced the medical resources devoted to treating the disease. The implication is that advances in medical technology have the potential to either increase or decrease the demand for medical resources. Overall, advances in technology have probably increased the demand for medical resources over the past several decades. It is easy to assume that this trend will persist into the near future.

Trends in the general economy can affect the demand for medical services and resources. During a severe recession, demand decreases as the unemployed lose their health benefits. However, during the early stages of recession, demand may increase slightly as furloughed workers who retain their health benefits increase their utilization of health services. The current economic recovery should result in an increase in the demand for medical services and resources.

Family income is related to utilization of medical resources. The number of visits to physicians tends to decrease slightly with decreased income level. Hospital discharges per 1,000 persons and length of stay decrease with increases in family income. Most studies have not found a strong relationship between family income and the dollar value of total medical services utilized.[3] However, expenditures for physicians' services increase with family income. These findings suggest that the resource intensity of a visit to a physician tends to be greater at higher family income levels. Consequently, as family incomes increase because of the improving economy and because of increased productivity, the demand for physicians' services is likely to expand somewhat in the near term.

There are a number of demographic factors which are related to the utilization of medical services and resources. These include the population growth rate, age distribution, sex composition, racial composition, educational level, and migration patterns.

If other factors remain constant, a growing population results in a growing demand for physicians' services and a growing level of health care expenditures. A recent study found that population growth accounted for about 19 percent of the $12.7 billion (in 1979 dollars) increase in annual payments to physicians between 1970 and 1979.[4] Furthermore, it is clear that the growth of the population during the decade of the

1970s had a substantial impact on the growth of total health expenditures since total personal health care expenditures increased 15 percentage points more than per capita personal health care expenditures.

The magnitude of the impact of population growth on health care expenditures and on the demand for physicians' services is likely to diminish in the future because the growth rate of the U.S. population is slowing. According to Bureau of the Census estimates and recent projections: (1) during the 1970s, the population grew 11 percent; (2) in the 1980s, the population will grow 9.6 percent; and (3) during the 1990s, the population is likely to grow only 7.3 percent. It is projected that after 1999, the population growth rate will slow even further.[5]

Utilization of health care services is strongly related to the age distribution of the population. For males, the average number of physician visits first decreases with age and later begins to increase with age. For females, the average number of physician visits tends to increase with age. Other studies have found that adults undergo more surgery than do children, but children are more likely to see specialists and utilize preventive care services.

Hospital utilization shows a different pattern. When hospitalization for childbirth is removed from the analysis, hospital discharges and lengths of stay increase as the population ages. This pattern reflects the more serious health care needs of the elderly.

Age distribution is also related to the use of certain specialists' services. AMA data indicate that in 1978, over 60 percent of the patients of the typical office-based physician were either under age fifteen or were sixty-five and older. In 1978, these two categories comprised only about 32 percent of the total population.

Likely changes in the age composition between 1985 and the end of the century include: (1) the percentage of the population under age eighteen will decrease from 26.3 percent to about 25.1 percent; (2) the percentage of the population aged thirty to forty-four years will increase from 21.8 percent to about 23.4 percent; (3) the percentage of the population sixty-five years and older will increase from 11.9 percent to about 13.0 percent; and (4) the percentage of the population eighty-five years and older will increase from 1.1 percent to about 1.8 percent.

In the near future, the largest absolute increase in population, in the near future, will be in the age group thirty to forty-four years. It will rise from about 51.9 million in 1985 to 59.9 million in 1990. In terms of growth rate, the fastest growing category will be the eighty-five and older age group which is expected to increase 82.7 percent, from 2.7 million people in 1985 to 4.9 million people by the year 2000. The population aged sixty-five and older, currently 28.6 million, is expected to reach about 34 million in 1995. From 1995 to 2005 this age group will grow slowly. After 2010, the number of those sixty-five and older will grow rapidly as the "baby boom" generation reaches retirement age. By 2025, this age group is likely to number 58.8 million persons, which will be approximately 19.5 percent of the population.[6]

Females utilize more health care services than do males. National Center for Health Statistics data[7] indicate that in 1980: (1) the typical female had an average of 5.4 physician visits compared with 4.0 for males; (2) the average number of discharges from short-stay hospitals per 100 persons was 15.8 for females and 11.9 for males; and (3) 12.1 percent of females had at least one short-stay hospital episode compared with 8.6 percent of males.

However, females typically had shorter stays in hospitals (6.8 days) than males (8.8 days). In part, the higher utilization by females is related to childbearing. Even when this is considered, however, females still typically utilize more health care services than do males.

The number of males per 100 females has been decreasing throughout this century. There were approximately 104 males per 100 females in 1900; by 1980 this ratio had fallen to about 94.5 males per 100 females. However, the really large change in sex composition has been among the elderly. In the sixty-five and older group, there were 102 males per 100 females in 1900 compared with about 68 males per 100 females in 1980.

In the sixty-five and older category, the number of males is likely to increase from 10.3 million in 1980 to 13.8 million in 2000, a 34 percent increase. Over the same period, the number of elderly females is likely to increase from 15.2 million to 21.6 million, a 42 percent increase. Consequently, the number of males to 100 females in the older age groups will continue to decrease slightly.

Some variation in utilization patterns still exists across racial or ethnic groups, although these differences have narrowed in recent decades:[8] (1) relative to blacks, whites have more physician visits and see a physician more frequently; (2) whites are more likely to have office or telephone visits, while blacks are more likely to see a physician in a hospital emergency room or clinic setting; (3) relative to blacks, whites are more likely to see physicians for preventive care; and (4) blacks tend to utilize hospital resources more intensively than do whites.

The racial composition of the U.S. population has been changing rapidly and is likely to continue to change. Bureau of the Census projections[9] suggest that this trend will continue into the future:

Year	Composition of the U.S. Population
1982	16.9 nonwhites per 100 whites.
1990	18.4 nonwhites per 100 whites.

2000   20.3 nonwhites per 100 whites.
2050   29.9 nonwhites per 100 whites.
2080   34.2 nonwhites per 100 whites.

The educational level of the head of the household is another demographic characteristic that is strongly related to utilization of health
resources:[10] (1) utilization of physicians' services by males increases
with educational level, but there is less variation among females; (2)
physician visits tend to increase with educational level even when family
income is held constant; and (3) the higher the educational level, the
more likely that a person will have had a physician visit in the preceding
year.

The higher the educational level, the more likely a telephone visit
and the less likely that the visit will occur in a clinic or emergency
room. Furthermore, the higher the level of education, the more likely
that the patient will see a specialist and the higher the percentage of
preventive care visits.

Hospital utilization also varies with educational level. The higher the
educational level, the fewer hospital discharges per 1,000 persons, and
the shorter the average length of hospital stay. However, although some
utilization measures tend to decrease as the level of education increases,
studies indicate that expenditures for health care increase with the level
of education.[11]

The level of educational attainment in the United States has been
rising; the median school years completed in 1980 by persons over
twenty-five years of age was 12.5 compared with 10.6 years of education
in 1960. This trend will probably continue.

In summary, the U.S. population will increase moderately from 1986
to 2000. Within this population, the number of thirty-three to forty-
four year olds will grow most rapidly, followed by those over sixty-five.
Since females use more services than males, whites more than blacks,
older people more than younger, and the educated more than the
uneducated, demand will continue to increase moderately until the year
2000.

Insurance Coverage

Studies have consistently found that the characteristics of health
insurance coverage, including the type of payee, extent of coverage, and
method of payment, influence the demand for medical services. Research
findings include:[12] (1) individuals with health insurance use more physicians' services than those without coverage; (2) insured individuals
use more physicians' services per disability day; (3) individuals with

hospital insurance have higher admission rates, especially low-income insured families; (4) regardless of income, individuals without insurance coverage have longer stays in hospitals; and (5) rates of surgery are higher for the insured population.

The findings of a recent study of the effects of different levels of cost sharing in health insurance are consistent with the view that the characteristics of health insurance affect demand.[13] Findings include: (1) per capita total expenditures for inpatient plus ambulatory services rise steadily as the coinsurance rate falls; (2) the number of ambulatory visits per person increases as the coinsurance rate decreases; (3) the probability of a visit to a physician or a hospital admission increases as the coinsurance rate decreases; (4) expenditures for adults show greater responsiveness to variation in cost sharing than do expenditures for children; and (5) different income groups have relatively similar utilization responses to cost sharing in health insurance.

These findings all suggest that the expansion of health insurance coverage over the past several decades has contributed significantly to the increased demand for medical services.

The number of individuals covered by private health insurance has increased substantially in recent decades.[14] Between 1965 and 1982, the number of individuals with coverage for hospital or surgical expense increased 38 percent, while the number with coverage for physicians' expense increased 57 percent. Over this same period, the number of individuals with major medical coverage increased 134 percent. The proportion of personal health expenditures paid by private insurance also increased from 32.7 percent in 1965 to 40.5 percent in 1982.

The number of individuals covered by federal, state, and local health care programs has also increased over the past several decades. For example, the number of individuals enrolled in Medicare (hospital and/ or medical insurance) increased from 19.5 million in 1967 to 29.0 million in 1981, a 48.7 percent increase. Over this same period, Medicare benefit payments increased 855 percent. The percentage of national health expenditures paid by all levels of government increased from 36.8 percent in 1967 to 42.4 percent in 1982.

A number of factors suggest that further changes in the characteristics of health insurance and benefit programs will occur and that these changes will tend to slow the rate of growth of demand for medical care services and resources. These factors include:

- The trend for corporations to provide less generous health benefits for their employees is likely to continue; foreign competition and economic uncertainty are forcing corporations to cut back on the benefits they provide to their employees.

- Limits on the amount of tax-free health benefits businesses can provide to their employees are being discussed in some government circles; the effect of this tax policy would be to induce employees to choose less generous and less expensive insurance programs.
- The number of individuals covered by health insurance and benefit programs is likely to grow more slowly in the future since the growth rate of the population is slowing and a high percentage of the population is already covered by health programs.
- Further cuts in the Medicaid and Medicare programs are likely because of the continuing budget problems of the federal government.
- Eligibility standards for government health benefit programs are likely to be tightened even further in order to reduce governmental outlays for health.

Hence, the demand for health services in the future may decrease as the breadth of insurance coverage narrows and the requirement for a larger copayment by the consumer is firmly established.

Accessibility of Services

As medical resources become more accessible, the time and travel associated with consuming medical care decrease and, consequently, demand tends to increase, that is, an increase in the supply of physicians in a geographic area tends to increase the quantity of physicians' services utilized by the population in that area because the increased supply makes it more convenient to see a physician. In general, the greater the physician-to-population ratio the shorter are waiting times for appointments, the shorter are waiting times in the physician's office, the shorter the travel to the physician's office, and the more convenient are the physician's office hours for patients.

With the exception of hospital resources, projections indicate that the supply of medical care resources is likely to continue to grow faster than the population. As accessibility improves because of this trend, demand is likely to expand slightly.

Migration has also influenced the demand for services. Historically, migrants have tended to be young adults. Therefore, an area experiencing in-migration would have a shift in the age distribution of the population in a direction that would increase the demand for obstetric care. However, the elderly are also migrating. In four of the five fastest growing states in the 1970–1980 period (Nevada, Arizona, Florida, Wyoming, and Utah), the rate of growth of the sixty-five and older population exceeded the national growth rate for that group. This suggests that many of the rapidly growing areas in the United States will experience increasing demand for physicians' services, particularly in the specialties of internal medicine, radiology, rehabilitation medicine, and surgery, or those services utilized by the elderly.

In the future, states in the South and West will continue to see a growing demand for physicians' services. Correspondingly, physicians will migrate to these areas to provide services to meet the demand.

Future Trends in Demand

A general implication of the changes discussed here is that it is likely there will be some instability in the demand for physicians' services in some specialty groups and in some geographic areas. This reflects the following:

1. If inflation-adjusted physician services expenditures continue to increase, the public is likely to focus more on physician services expenditures as a cost problem and decrease its demand.
2. The shifting age composition of the population is likely to create shifts in the demand for physicians' services by specialty. For example, the number of births may increase slightly between now and 1990 because of the changing age composition of women. However, after the mid-1990s, the number of births will be below the current level of 3.7 million per year. Therefore, the demand for obstetric and pediatric care is likely to increase slightly in the near future, but the increase will only be temporary.
3. The increasing number of the elderly suggests that demand is likely to grow for the services of internists, radiologists, surgeons, and general/family practitioners. This growth in demand should not be overestimated since the sixty-five and older group will grow only about 22 percent between 1985 and the year 2000. The really rapid growth of the elderly will not occur until the next century.
4. The increasing proportion of the elderly in the population may have adverse implications for the demand for the services of office-based psychiatrists since less than 10 percent of their patients are in the sixty-five and older category. Again, large impacts are not likely to occur until the next century.
5. The changing sex composition of the elderly is likely to intensify concerns over the costs of long-term care. As the sex composition of the elderly changes, the likelihood increases that a higher proportion of the elderly will live alone and will need nursing home care because family support services are inadequate. Phy-

sicians may face an increased demand for house calls from this age group.

6. The changing sex composition of the population may also increase the demand for the services of general/family practitioners and internists. These two specialty groups treat a high proportion of female patients as well as a high proportion of elderly patients.

7. If the current differences in utilization patterns persist and other factors do not change, the likely impacts of projected changes in racial composition could include a slight decrease in demand for physician visits, an increasing proportion of physician visits in clinic settings, a decreasing proportion of preventive care visits, and an increase in hospital utilization.

8. The migration patterns of the U.S. population suggest that growth in demand for physicians' services is likely to vary substantially from area to area. In general, states in the West will experience rapid growth while states in the Northeast will experience slow growth in demand.

9. A shift in the locale in which physician services are provided from the hospital setting to the office setting is occurring secondary to Medicare's prospective payment system. Since it is not clear that a shift in the location in which services are delivered will be more efficient, increased political pressure for physician-inclusive DRGs may result.

10. Since the demand for medical resources will most likely grow more slowly than the supply of medical resources, the level of economic competition in the medical care sector will intensify.

Public Attitudes

In addition to the demand factors discussed in the preceding section, public attitudes influence the delivery of health services, and shifts in attitudes herald significant impacts on physicians and their practices.

While the AMA has conducted public attitude surveys for thirty years, an in-depth analysis of these surveys began in 1977. In general, these surveys have demonstrated that the public is dissatisfied with and distrustful of the medical profession as a whole, but individuals are reasonably pleased with their personal physician(s).[15]

As interest in public attitudes toward physicians has increased, a number of efforts to improve the image of physicians have been initiated. Since many of these efforts have been compilations of baseline survey data against which to evaluate program success, the AMA decided to conduct baseline public opinion surveys in each of the fifty states to serve as a cornerstone for continuing communications activities.

During July 1985 telephone interviews with 400 randomly selected adults in each of the fifty states (a total of 20,000 interviews) were conducted by Kane, Parsons, Inc. and V. Lance Tarrance and Associates. Although no questions were asked of a truly national sample, national findings can be closely approximated by weighting each of the 20,000 state responses with the ratio of the state to national population and aggregating.

Table 3.1 presents and compares the 1985 national data with earlier results wherever possible. The table also includes a column showing the number of percentage points between the highest and lowest state findings on each question, indicating dissimilarity in results across the various states.

The principal findings of the 1985 data are:

The earlier longstanding deterioration in the public image of physicians has ended and there are strong indications of an upturn in key dimensions. As shown in Table 3.1, positive responses to ten of thirteen statements about physicians have increased in the last year and, in some cases, have increased substantially. There are several plausible explanations.

First, many state, county, and specialty societies have undertaken major programs to improve the image of physicians. It is likely that these efforts are beginning to have some impact. Second, there are additional signs that the profession of medicine is being viewed by the public in a more realistic light.

However, this set of findings should be examined in the context of the rather poor ratings at which many of these indicators have leveled off. In addition, several key questions continue to show declines. Thus, while the overall picture is encouraging, there is still much room for improvement.

The second major finding from the 1985 state data concerns the public's growing uncertainty about professional liability issues. The AMA has trended three basic questions on this issue since 1982. The percentage of respondents who answered "don't know" or "not sure" to these questions is indicated in Table 3.2.

These three questions show a strong trend toward increasing uncertainty over time. In fact, the percentage of "don't know" responses doubled in each case during the last year and now represent sizable proportions of the total population.

As described earlier, the "Difference Across States" column in Table 3.1 presents a measure of the variance in responses to a particular question across states. It is the difference in "agree" responses between the highest and lowest state on that question. Because of the sample sizes involved, a difference of seven points is necessary to assume that the highest and lowest states do actually differ on a specific question.

The data indicate that of thirty-two questions asked, every question varies significantly across states. Responses to six questions vary by more than 20 percent; responses to a question about the community involvement of physicians differ by 34 points.

These data show that public attitudes toward physicians, professional liability, and access to care among the poor and elderly are very different in each state. There is strong agreement that medical science is effective, that physicians are up to date technologically, and that doctors are interested in patients.

Supply of Physicians

Physicians who practice in the United States come predominantly from U.S. medical schools. The majority of graduates of U.S. schools enter a graduate medical education program following receipt of a medical degree. The public perception in the mid-1960s of an impending shortage of physicians prompted the establishment of forty new medical schools. The result was a doubling of the medical school class size with a sharp increase in the number of graduates (Table 3.3).

In 1975 the AMA House of Delegates accepted the integration of the first post-M.D. year of graduate medical education with subsequent years. As a result, freestanding internship programs were no longer approved and the total number of graduate medical education programs decreased. However, the number of trainees in graduate programs increased, partly as a result of the increase in the number of U.S. medical school graduates (Table 3.3).

Concurrently with the increase in U.S. graduates, a second stream of new physicians contributed to the manpower pool: graduates of foreign medical schools (FMGs), many of whom were born outside the United States. Table 3.4 shows the number of U.S. citizen FMG residents from 1979–1980 to 1984–1985.

Foreign medical graduates must be certified by the Educational Commission for Foreign Medical Graduates (ECFMG) to be eligible for appointment to a residency program. Table 3.5 provides data on the number of persons certified by ECFMG each year. The new examination for foreign medical school graduates, called the Foreign Medical Graduate Examination in the Medical Sciences (FMGEMS), was first administered in 1984. The pass rate for the 21,026 who took both parts of the examination was 15.6 percent.

U.S. citizens who took both days numbered 3,520 and had a pass rate for both days of 4.6 percent. Foreign nationals who took both days numbered 17,506 and had a pass rate for both days of 17.8 percent. These numbers include individuals who were repeating the exam. The pass rate for individuals taking both parts of the examination for the first time was even lower.

Many FMGs take part in the National Resident Matching Program. The number of these applicants increased from about 3,074 in 1975 to more than 5,948 in 1985. The success rate of all FMGs in the MATCH decreased from 34 percent in 1975 to 27 percent in 1985 (Table 3.7) with an increase in the absolute number matched.

The number of USFMGs participating in the MATCH increased from 536 in 1981 to 1,692 in 1985 (Table 3.8).

In contrast, the number of foreign national FMGs participating in the MATCH increased from 1,143 in 1980 to 4,256 in 1985. Of these, 645 matched in 1980 (56 percent) and 918 or 22 percent matched in 1985 (Table 3.9).

The number of FMGs entering the first year of residency training, however, is not directly related to the number who successfully match. This reflects the fact that some individuals obtain positions outside the MATCH or after the MATCH is completed. Tables 2.5, 2.6, and 2.7 show the trends in numbers of FMGs, USFMGs, and foreign national FMGs entering the first year of residency. It is important to note that the number of all first-year FMGs decreased by 373 in 1985 from the number in 1984. Three-fourths of this decrease was found in the USFMG group. There is growing competition between U.S. and foreign graduates for positions.

Following completion of residency training, FMGs seek licensure. The number of FMGs obtaining an initial license in at least one state increased from 1,419 in 1960 to 5,965 in 1975. The number decreased after 1975 to 3,131 in 1981 and increased again in 1982 and 1983 but decreased to 4,094 in 1984 (Table 3.5).

The percentage of FMGs in the U.S. physician population has increased steadily from 17.1 percent in 1970 to 21.6 percent in 1983. Active physicians who are FMGs have increased from 17.8 percent in 1970 to 22.4 percent in 1983 (Table 3.10).

Within the FMG population 81.9 percent were in patient care, more than two-thirds (67.5 percent) of whom were in an office-based practice. Two-thirds (66.6 percent) of active FMGs were practicing in anesthesiology, internal medicine, general practice, general surgery, obstetrics/gynecology, pathology, pediatrics, or psychiatry.

In summary, the health care delivery system of the United States is affected by two streams of physician manpower. One consists of the graduates of the 127 U.S. medical schools and the other consists of graduates from a variety of foreign medical schools. In the FMG stream, there are a significant number of Americans and their numbers appear to be growing. This portends increased competition with U.S. graduates for residency positions in the future and raises once again questions about the adequacy of the educational experience of these individuals. It also portends another round of destabilizing political battles as disappointed FMGs, especially U.S. citizens, are unable to enter the profession through residency training programs.

Number of Physicians in the United States

Information on the number of physicians in the United States is taken from the AMA Physician Masterfile. This file includes all physicians who have met the educational standards for primary recognition as physicians. The names of graduates of U.S. medical schools are entered into the Masterfile when the M.D. degree has been awarded. Names of the graduates of foreign medical schools who reside in the United States are incorporated into the Masterfile when they qualify to enter a graduate medical education program accredited by the Accreditation Council on Graduate Medical Education (ACGME).

Every four years, all physicians listed in the Masterfile are surveyed to obtain current information on the physician's professional activity. The primary professional activity of an individual is determined on the basis of hours reportedly spent in patient care or other professional activities. The specialty of practice is determined by the reported hours devoted to patient care in the specialty. The primary activity (and the primary specialty) is the one to which the physician devotes the greatest amount of time.

Tables 3.11, 3.12, and 3.13 show trends in the size of the physician population and in the type of activity of U.S. physicians for the eighteen-year period of 1965–1983.

The number of active physicians has increased 73 percent since 1965. The number of physicians providing patient care has increased 63 percent, while the number in other professional activities such as administration, medical teaching, and research has increased 139 percent.

Most striking is the 330 percent increase in the number of physicians who designate research as their primary activity. The exact meaning of this remains unclear, but the increase undoubtedly reflects the growth in medical school faculties during the expansion of the medical school enterprise.

Most physicians who are involved in medical teaching are also providing patient care. This may explain why the number who designate teaching as their major activity is unusually low. U.S. medical schools reported 44,984 full-time clinical faculty in 1985. This is almost six times the number of physicians who identify medical teaching as their major activity.[16]

Physician Work Patterns

Historically, the organizational structure of medical practice was simple. The typical physician functioned as an independent, solo, fee-for-service practitioner whose work centered in the office. Although the physician may have treated patients in a hospital setting, medical practice was usually independent of the hospital. In essence, the economic structure of the physician's medical practice was similar to that of a small, independent "businessman."

Over the past several decades the structure of medical practice has become more complex and diverse. It has become more difficult to categorize a physician's practice, since many physicians practice in more than one type of setting. With regard to business decisions, the practicing physician has become less of an independent entrepreneur. Increasingly, the physician practices in an environment where business decisions are made by nonphysicians or are strongly influenced by nonphysicians.

The growth of group practice has been dramatic. Group practice is defined as the application of medical services by three or more physicians formally organized to provide medical care, consultation, diagnosis, and/or treatment through the joint use of equipment and personnel, and with the income from medical practice distributed in accordance with methods previously determined by members of the group. Between 1969 and 1980 the number of group practices increased 70 percent, while the number of physician positions in medical groups more than doubled.[17] Between 1980 and 1984 the number of group practices increased another 40 percent and the number of physician positions in a group setting increased almost 60 percent.[18] By 1984 approximately 35 percent of all active, nonfederal physicians were affiliated with a group practice.

Recently, an increasing number of physicians are accepting salaried positions. This phenomenon is much more common among recent graduates than it is among older physicians. Physicians with five or fewer years of practice are two-and-one-half times as likely as physicians with eleven or more years of experience to be salaried (26.8 percent versus 9.3 percent, respectively).[19] The extent to which young physicians are driven into salaried positions by competitive forces and whether they may be taking these jobs only temporarily to gain entry into the market is unclear.

A growing number of physicians are providing services through alternative delivery mechanisms, such as health maintenance organizations (HMOs), hospital clinics, and freestanding emergency centers. As of December 1983 there were 290 operating HMOs serving an enrolled population of 13.6 million. Of these, 190 were group or staff-type HMOs, providing care in their own centralized facilities—frequently only to prepaid members. The remaining 100 were independent practice associations (IPAs) in which physicians practice in their private offices and are reimbursed on a fee-for-service basis by the IPA, which in turn receives its payment through monthly capitation. By the end of 1984, 337 HMO plans serving 16,742,000 members were identified by Interstudy.[20] The rate of growth in enrollment over the previous twelve-month period was a record 23 percent. The greatest increases were experienced by young plans (less than five years), small plans (fewer than 50,000 enrollees), and IPA type plans. In 1984 an AMA survey enumerated 27,630 physicians in group practices with at least some business on a prepaid basis.

A new form of health plan known as the preferred provider organization (PPO) has recently appeared in numerous states. A PPO is a group of hospitals and physicians which contracts with employers, insurance carriers, and third-party administrators to provide comprehensive medical services to subscribers on a discounted fee-for-service basis. One-fifth of all physicians with five or fewer years of experience have a contract with a PPO compared with 18.7 percent of physicians with six to ten years of experience, and 14.3 of those with eleven or more years of experience.[21]

The degree to which medical practice has become integrated with the hospital is also significant. Excluding residents, 8.9 percent of nonfederal, patient care physicians were full-time hospital employees during 1984.[22] Many physicians who are not actually employed by hospitals have become economically integrated with hospitals. Approximately one-fourth of all nonfederal patient care physicians, including residents, have a financial arrangement with hospitals.[23]

Little change occurred from 1983 to 1984 with respect to the amount of time physicians spent on professional activities. Declining patient demand per physician was apparently offset by increases in the time spent with each patient and presumably a concurrent improvement in public attitudes toward physicians. During 1984, mean work hours among physicians ranged from a low of 51.1 hours per week among psychiatrists to a high of 59.6 hours among anesthesiologists. Mean work load was greatest among rural, self-employed, solo-practice physicians. The "average" physician in 1984 worked 56.8 hours per week, of which 25 hours were spent in the office, 8.4 hours on hospital rounds, and 5.8 hours performing surgery.

In contrast to the stability of total time spent in professional activities, there has been some reallocation of time across activities. The impact of DRGs and the growing role of alternative health care delivery systems is clearly reflected in this shift. In particular, the average number of hours spent on hospital rounds per week in 1984 was down 11.6 percent from 1983. All major medical specialties experienced declines in hours spent on hospital rounds, the rate of decline ranging from 4.6 percent for obstetricians/gynecologists to 15.5 percent for general and family practitioners. For all physicians, office hours and hours spent performing inpatient surgery were also down 3.8 percent and 3.3 percent, respectively. In contrast to the decline in time spent in the office and with hospital inpatients, time spent seeing patients in hospital outpatient departments, emergency rooms, and other settings increased. This increase was sufficient to cause the total amount of time in direct patient care activities to remain constant.[24]

The declines in patient visits, hospital discharges, and lengths of hospital stays were notable trends in medical practice during 1984. The increasing physician-to-population ratio and the new prospective payment system appear to be major factors contributing to reduced utilization levels.

The average number of total patient visits for all physicians declined 4.5 percent in 1984. The decrease in utilization was manifest in every specialty, census division, type of practice, location, employment status, and physician age group. Obstetricians/gynecologists experienced the greatest decline (7.9 percent) in total patient visits, while surgeons had the smallest decline (1.2 percent). Physicians in a group practice achieved a higher level of total visits than solo practitioners. Self-employed physicians reported more patient visits per week (124.9) and a smaller decrease in the number of patient visits (3.9 percent) than employee physicians in 1984.

The average number of patients discharged from the hospital decreased 4 percent during 1984. All specialties experienced sharp declines, ranging from 3.2 percent for surgeons to 10.9 percent among general/family practitioners.[25]

In summary, it is clear that major shifts are occurring in the way physicians practice. Increasing numbers are salaried and/or have relationships with a prepaid plan of some form. These changes are reflected in the number of patients seen, the location in which patients are seen, and the types of visits that occur.

Physician Fees, Income, and Expenses

Information presented in this section draws heavily on the work of Daniel J. Duann and Sara L. Thran.[26]

Annual Net Income. In 1984 the average net income (after expenses, but before taxes) of physicians was $108,400. This figure includes contributions to pension, profit-sharing, and deferred compensation plans. It represents the average income for active nonfederal patient care physicians, excluding residents. The level of income in 1984 represented an increase of 2 percent over 1983. This is considerably lower than the 6.8 percent growth rate of 1982–1983. Furthermore, physicians' incomes increased less than the rate of inflation in 1984. Thus, the purchasing power or "real earnings" of physicians actually declined in 1984.

There were variations in the levels and percentage changes in physicians' net incomes by specialty and location. Among the specialties, surgeons had the highest average net income ($151,800), while general and family practitioners had the lowest ($71,100). Physicians in the East South Central census division had the highest average net income ($122,200), while physicians in New England had the lowest average income ($87,300). Physicians in the Mountain census division enjoyed the highest growth rate in net income (11.9 percent) in 1984. On the other hand, average net income of physicians in the East North Central and West South Central divisions declined 4.3 percent in that year. Average net income is higher for self-employed physicians ($118,600) than for employee physicians ($80,400); in 1984 earnings grew more slowly for self-employed physicians (2.3 percent) than for employee physicians (3.6 percent) (Tables 3.14–3.16).

Physician Fees. In 1984, the fee for a visit to a physician was about $26, compared with about $11 in 1974, and $17 in 1979. Significant variations in physicians' fees exist depending on the specialty, geographic location, kind of practice, and age of the practitioner. Hypothetically, the lowest fee would have been charged by a solo family practitioner, sixty-six years of age or older, practicing in a rural area of Mississippi (or another East South Central state), while the highest fee would have been charged for a single visit to an obstetrician/gynecologist in a non-solo practice in New York City (or another city with a population of over 1 million in one of the Middle Atlantic states). This hypothetical family practitioner would have charged about $17.50; the obstetrician would have charged about $36.50, or twice as much.

In 1974 also, the hypothetical family practitioner would have charged the lower mean fee ($8.75), and the obstetrician/gynecologist the highest ($13). In that year also, physicians in the East South Central states would have reported the lowest mean fees ($9.24), while physicians in the Middle Atlantic states would have reported the highest ($12.60). Physicians in solo practice reported lower fees than physicians in non-solo practice, physicians in nonmetropolitan areas reported lower fees than those in metropolitan areas, and those in metropolitan areas of 1 million or more reported the highest fees of all. Table 3.15 shows the mean fee for an office visit with an established patient for 1974–1976, 1978–1980, and 1983–1984.[27]

Physicians charge different fees for initial visits and for follow-up hospital visits. The mean fee for visits with a new patient in 1984 for all physicians was $47.21. Internists charged the highest mean fee for an initial visit in 1984, i.e., $71.00. Internists in the Pacific states charged the highest fee of all for a first visit, $93.15; the family practitioner in a rural area charged the least, $23.76.

Follow-up visits in hospitals tend to command somewhat higher fees than regular visits to a physician's office but these fees are still considerably less than initial visits. The mean fee in 1984 for hospital follow-up visits was $29.00; the lowest fees were reported by surgeons in the Mountain States, $21.23.

Physician Expenses. Physician expenses over the past ten years have shown substantial increases. In 1974 the mean professional expense for all physicians was $34,000 and in 1984, it was $92,600 (Table 3.16). As with fees, there are differences in expenses among specialties, among different geographic locations, age groups, and types of practice. Among locations, the lowest expenses for 1984 were reported in New England ($65,100) and the highest in the West South Central states ($116,300). As in earlier years, surgeons had the highest expenses ($131,200) and pediatricians the lowest ($78,200). Physicians in solo practice had a lower average level of professional expenses ($84,600) than physicians in non-solo practice ($105,200). Physicians in nonmetropolitan areas had the lowest expenses in 1984 ($84,900); those in metropolitan areas with populations of less than 1 million had the highest expenses ($96,600).

Professional liability insurance continues to be a major part of total expenses. Premiums charged by one large multistate insurance company, St. Paul, in 1985 ranged from $1,365 in its lowest risk category in Arkansas to $92,570 in its highest risk category in Florida. These premiums purchased coverage of up to $1 million per claim and a total of $3 million for all claims. Obstetricians/gynecologists are in the highest risk category. Premiums vary by state, by coverage limits, and by company. Between 1984 and 1985, the major contributing factors to the increase in total expenses were professional liability insurance premiums, office expenses, and medical supply costs; the percentage increases for these items during 1984 were 18.3 percent, 14.3 percent, and 14.1 percent, respectively. These same factors contributed the most to the 9.6 percent increase in expenses between 1982 and 1983.

Financial Arrangements with Hospitals. As noted earlier, about one-fourth of physicians, excluding residents and physicians in federal employment, have some kind of financial arrangement with a hospital. There are primarily three kinds of arrangements: salary, fee-for-service, and percentage of department revenue. Younger physicians are more likely to have financial arrangements than older ones, and women more likely than men. Analysis of the data by physician income suggests that the percentage of physicians with hospital arrangements increases as income levels increase up to an income level of $100,000, but such arrangements decrease among physicians with incomes over $100,000 as income rises (Table 3.17).

Overall, physicians without hospital financial arrangements earn both larger average net incomes and more income from hospital inpatient services than do physicians with such arrangements. However, an agreement with a hospital does not appear to affect the fee charged for a hospital visit.

Physicians with financial arrangements with hospitals appear to spend more time making hospital rounds than physicians who do not have such arrangements. Furthermore, their patients appear to have longer hospital stays than those of physicians without such arrangements.

Medicare Participation. Medicare's "participating physician" program took effect on 1 October 1985. This program (part of the Deficit Reduction Act of 1984) encourages physicians to accept assignment (i.e., accept whatever the federal government provides for a given service) for a one-year period for all services provided to elderly patients. Those who choose not to participate may continue to assign Medicare claims on a case-by-case basis. In addition, the 1984 Act imposes a freeze on allowable fees reimbursed by Medicare. The freeze includes unassigned claims from nonparticipating physicians, that is, claims from recipients who have been billed directly by their physician.

The intent is to encourage increased assignment of claims to Medicare and to reduce federal outlays. The extension of the fee freeze to unassigned claims is designed to discourage shifting the burden of financing health care to elderly recipients. About 37 percent of all physicians have agreed to the Medicare Participant Physician Program. There are differences in participation rates across specialties and previous assignment rates. There are lower participation rates for physicians with specialty board certification, and lower participation rates for physicians in rural areas. Probably the primary factor influencing participation is economic: participation is more likely for physicians who had previously assigned a larger percentage of patients and to physicians whose usual fees were relatively close to the Medicare prevailing fee.

Professional Liability

Professional liability significantly influences the quality, availability, and cost of physician services. At issue is the right of the individual to utilize the judicial system to redress a wrong. Year by year, the number of suits, the size of claims, and the number and size of awards have increased.

A 1969 report noted that total premiums paid by physicians for professional liability in 1968 was $75 million.[28] The report also stated that since World War II, premium rates have risen at more than three times the cost of living. Underwriting losses on this line of insurance have been reported since 1959.

In 1979, the Health Care Financing Administration reported that a survey of premium rates found an average premium increase of 168 percent for the period of 1974–1977.[29] Part of this increase was attributed to the growing number of physicians purchasing higher limits of coverage.

In 1980, the National Association of Insurance Commissioners reported on the analysis of 71,782 professional liability closed claims from July 1975 through 1978.[30] During this period, the average award per injury increased 70 percent with inflation accounting for 28 percent of the increase.

The report noted that a major factor in the growth of indemnity was the rising number of large settlements or judgments with a 13 percent increase in indemnity payments of $50,000 or more in 1975 and a 20 percent increase in 1978. In 1975, only five awards of $1 million or more were reported while twenty-three were reported in 1978.

More recent information indicates a continuation of the earlier trends. The AMA Socioeconomic Monitoring System compared the number of malpractice claims by selected characteristics.[31] The results are shown in Table 3.18.

Premium costs have continued to rise. Several sources[32] were used to estimate the following ranges for total direct premiums paid by physicians:

Year	*Premiums*
1982	$1.43 to $1.47 billion
1983	$1.645 to $1.75 billion
1984	$2.7 to $3.0 billion
1985	$3.4 to $3.48 billion

An American Hospital Association (AHA) study indicated that in 1984 $1.8 billion was spent by 60 to 80 percent of U.S. hospitals for direct premiums for professional liability coverage. According to the AHA, of this amount, two-thirds to three-quarters should be allocated to physicians according to the AHA. In addition, $200 million was spent in 1984 for hospital self-insured coverage and coverage insured outside the United States, bringing total hospital costs for coverage to an estimated $2 billion.

As noted above, the number and cost of claims have increased more rapidly for surgical specialists than for nonsurgical specialists. The increase has been especially marked for obstetricians related to claims on behalf of newborn children.

A survey of premiums for physicians practicing obstetrics conducted by the American College of Obstetrics and Gynecology[33] confirms that these are rising rapidly and in one area the annual premium has reached $144,000. The inability of some obstetricians to obtain coverage at any cost has been reported.

Results of Liability Crisis. Many physicians have responded to the increased frequency of claims by practicing "defensive medicine." This involves the performance of additional tests or procedures, not because they are judged to be necessary, but to avoid an accusation of negligence. Another form of defensive medicine occurs when the physician avoids certain procedures, even when they may be medically indicated, because legal risks may arise from potential complications. A survey concluded that 70 percent of physicians had adopted some defensive measures prior to 1984 and that 41.8 percent either increased the level of their defensive practices or adopted new measures in 1984.

Additional follow-up visits and increased record-keeping costs together amounted to an increase of $960 million in total health care costs in 1984. The survey indicated that the average physician increased record-keeping costs by 2.9 percent, prescribed 3.2 percent more tests and procedures, and increased follow-up visits by 2.6 percent. It was not possible to calculate from the information available the incremental costs for the prescription of additional tests and procedures. However, the total costs of the increased record-keeping and follow-up visits can be projected at $9.2 billion in 1984. The cost of increased time spent with patients is not included since that is a cost of good medicine, not of defensive measures. Therefore, a conservative estimate of the total costs for defensive measures in 1984 would be $17.5 billion.

One facet of the liability issue is the liability of manufacturers of medical products. Immunization is generally accepted as a beneficial procedure, and there are legal requirements for immunization of some groups such as schoolchildren. In 1984 a crisis was narrowly averted when manufacturers of vaccines considered discontinuing the production of these materials because of their potential liability for untoward reactions. Recent information from Lederle suggests another crisis will occur in 1986.

Physicians are not alone in their concern over liability. Cities and counties have encountered huge increases in the cost of liability coverage and corporations have experienced difficulty in obtaining errors and omissions coverage for their directors. Successful suits have been filed against clergymen and law firms have noted large increases in the premiums for protection of members.

Although various explanations have been given for the increase in the number of claims and suits, proof of their relative importance is elusive. Consensus would seem to assign considerable importance to the increasing awareness of the public concerning the willingness of the courts to redress perceived injury and to invade the "deep pockets" of the insurance industry to protect an individual.

The increasing emphasis on reducing the cost of medical care must be considered a potential factor that may compromise the quality and results of professional services. To the extent that the Diagnostic Related Group (DRG) system limits resources available to the patient and encourages early discharge from the hospital, it offers the potential of increasing the risk to the patient and the liability of the physician.

Some lawyers have asserted that malpractice is the only cause of malpractice litigation. Medical societies, the organized medical staffs of hospitals, and licensing authorities have each increased their efforts to identify and counter the potential harm that may come from the practice of incompetent physicians. Aside from these efforts, evidence of the lessening of physician competence concomitant with the steady increase in litigation is lacking. Given the increasing length of the physician's education, efforts to eliminate the incompetent and the increasing scrutiny of a physician's practice, including peer review, general incompetence fails to explain the trends in malpractice litigation.

The increases in the number of claims and awards and in the size of awards will have significant effects on medical practice including the following:

- The costs of medical care will increase at a time when there is a concerted national effort to contain costs.
- Some medical specialty services may be less available as physicians alter their practices.
- The career choices of new physicians may be skewed in the direction of avoiding high-risk specialties and high-risk localities.
- Medical progress may be slowed by a reluctance to utilize new procedures associated with a high degree of legal liability.
- To the extent that physicians respond to the threat of malpractice by devoting more time to their patients and giving more thought to patient management, the quality of medical care may be enhanced.

Manpower

Market Forces

In 1981, a Board of Trustees report, *Health Manpower*, committed the AMA to a market-oriented approach when dealing with health manpower issues.[34] A 1984 board report re-emphasized this commitment and examined market effects on medical education.[35]

The market approach advocated by the AMA calls for decentralized decision-making in determining the flow of resources into the medical care delivery system. A wide range of individuals and institutions participates in the market for health manpower. For instance, individuals contemplating a career in medicine respond to future professional and economic prospects and to the relevant training costs of medical education. Private businesses and government as third-party payers make decisions that influence health manpower supply. Government also acts explicitly in the interest of the general public in a variety of ways, such as facilitating the financing of a medical education.

The market provides a self-adjusting mechanism which coordinates public demand for and the supply of health manpower. Adjustments in the market occur slowly due to the long lag between training and initiation of practice. Attempts to accelerate the adjustment process may circumvent needed adjustments and lead to undesirable supply outcomes. If freed from extensive regulation, the market for health manpower can help provide a cost-effective allocation of medical care.

Undergraduate and Graduate Medical Education

The market for undergraduate medical education has responded, albeit slowly, to the changing demand for physicians over the past two decades. In response to a perceived physician shortage in the 1960s, public policy provided support for expanding the number of and enrollment in medical schools. Financial assistance for medical students also was augmented. Partly as a result of these improved opportunities, first-year enrollment increased from 8,298 in the 1960-1961 academic year to 11,348 in 1970-1971 and to 17,204 in 1980-1981. Rapid expansion in first-year class size has, however, subsided and has actually declined slowly over the past three years. In addition, the first decline in the number of applicants to U.S. medical schools occurred in the 1982-1983 academic year and has continued.

Many policy-makers believe that the overall supply of physicians is now adequate and have acted to scale back medical school enrollment. One of these actions is the substitution of unsubsidized Health Education

Assistance Loans for federally subsidized scholarship and loan programs. Between the 1981-1982 and 1982-1983 academic years, funds for Guaranteed Student Loans and Health Professions Student Loans, the two main sources of subsidized loans for medical education, declined 19.9 percent and 5.7 percent, respectively. In addition, the Reagan Administration has recently proposed that no new funds be allocated for the National Health Service Corps or Health Professions Student Loan programs.

Direct state and federal support for medical schools has also declined in recent years. California has recently cut appropriations for its public medical schools. Federal support for teaching and training in medical schools, which reached a record $303 million (10 percent of the total medical school revenue) in 1974-1975, has declined to $232 million (3.2 percent) in 1981-1982.

Another market force now operating is the proposal to reduce or eliminate programs that provide financial assistance for U.S. citizens who study medicine overseas. The General Accounting Office in 1980 recommended additional scrutiny of offshore medical schools when granting financial aid to potential recipients. This recommendation was repeated again in 1985 and has been incorporated into a legislative proposal, commonly referred to as the Pepper Bill. Similar attempts to control the flow of U.S. citizens have come from the New York State Health Department which is examining the possibility of curbing the access of offshore students to clinical instruction in the state. Department officials believe that such clinical instruction reduces the number of available residency training positions in the state's teaching hospitals.

Market forces have also influenced graduate medical education in a number of ways. Teaching hospitals have independently chosen to slow the growth in the number of residency positions in recent years. The number of positions in 1978 was 63,163. This number rose to 68,217 in 1981, an annual average increase of 2.6 percent. Between 1981 and 1982, however, the number of residency positions increased only 1.4 percent to 69,142.

As stated in testimony before the Senate Finance Committee in 1985, the AMA supports the elimination of Medicare funding for alien foreign medical graduates. However, the AMA strongly supports international medical education exchanges but believes that other sources should be utilized to fund residency training for foreign students who are to return to their native countries for medical practice. The association also believes provision should be made to ensure an orderly transition for hospitals that rely on foreign medical graduates to meet patient care needs.

Market forces are beginning to have an appreciable effect on the rate of growth of the physician supply. Increased competition in medicine has also led to the diffusion of physicians into small towns and non-metropolitan areas. Due primarily to cost-containment efforts by government and businesses, the professional and economic prospects for the medical profession may be dimming. Individuals are bearing more of the costs of medical training as unsubsidized loans are being substituted for subsidized financial assistance. As a result of these trends, the rate of growth in the physician supply most likely will continue to decline.

Allied Health and Related Professions

The physician shortage after World War II continued into the 1960s. There was a need to extend physician services in order to adapt to the increasingly complex health care delivery system. The allied health professions proliferated and many of these new health professionals continue to be licensed through programs accredited by the AMA as a method of quality assurance to protect the public. Physician extenders, a product of the 1960s, were promoted to assure access to medical services in rural and inner-city areas. By 1985 there were 21,000 physicians' assistants licensed to practice in the United States, a number which has remained stable in the 1980s. In contrast, nurse practitioners, also a physician extender modality, have increased dramatically. The number of nurse practitioners certified by the American Nurses Association in 1985 will bring the total number of nurse practitioners to at least 40,000 and some estimates range as high as 100,000. Market forces which promoted the rise of physician extenders no longer exist. Increasing strife may, therefore, be inevitable between medicine and nursing regardless of the form(s) the health care delivery system takes.

Summary

Even to the most distant observer, it is clear that a major revolution in health care is occurring in the United States. That the accompanying changes are altering the professional life of physicians is equally obvious. Environmental changes, including fluctuations in the economy, changing demands for medical services, altered patterns of health insurance and copayments by subscribers, and the increasing accessibility of physicians have accelerated the changes that were initiated by the new reimbursement policies of the federal government.

While these trends were evolving, two streams of new physicians were entering the marketplace. These included the larger U.S. graduate stream and the smaller, but significant, FMG flow, including a progressively larger number of U.S. citizen FMGs.

Coupled with these upheavals has been a transformation of the health care delivery system leading to a host of new delivery forms including HMOs, IPAs, and PPAs.

These changes have modified the various characteristics of physician practices including gross and net income, expenses, hours of patient contact, location of health care delivery, liability concerns, and "business" arrangements with hospitals and for-profit health organizations.

It is suggested that much of this revolution represents "market forces" at work to tailor the system and its resources to the needs and demands of society.

Notes

The following individuals are recognized for their assistance in the preparation of this chapter: James L. Breeling; Katherine Chavigny, R.N., Ph.D.; Anne E. Crowley, Ph.D.; Richard L. Egan, M.D.; Charles W. Macenski, R.Ph.; Arthur M. Osteen, Ph.D.; and Frenando M. Trevino, Ph.D.

1. American Medical Association, Report of the Council on Long Range Planning and Development, "The Environment of Medicine" (Chicago: AMA, 1985).

2. Mark S. Freeland and Carol E. Schendler, "Health Spending in the 1980s: Integration of Clinical Practice Patterns with Management," *Health Care Financing Review*, Spring 1984, pp. 1–68.

3. Robert T. Dean et al., "An Analysis of Determinants of Health Care Utilization," Applied Management Sciences, Inc. and Bureau of Health Manpower, DHEW, 1980.

4. Dorothy P. Rice and Jacob J. Feldman, "Living Longer in the United States: Demographic Changes and Health Needs of the Elderly," *Milbank Memorial Fund Quarterly* 61 (Summer 1983): 362–396.

5. Bureau of the Census, "Projections of the Population of the United States: 1983 to 2080," Series P-25, Number 952, May 1984.

6. Bureau of the Census, "Projections."

7. National Center for Health Statistics, "Current Estimates from the National Health Interview Survey: United States, 1980," Series 10, Number 139, December 1981.

8. National Center for Health Statistics, "Physician Visits—Volume and Interval Since Last Visit: United States, 1975," Series 10, Number 128, April 1979.

9. Bureau of the Census, "Projections."

10. National Center for Health Statistics, "Physician Visits."

11. Dean et al., "Analysis of Determinants."

12. Jacqueline R. Leopold and Kathryn M. Langwell, "The Demand for Health Care with Special Emphasis on Cost Containment: A Review of the

Literature," *National Commission on the Cost of Medical Care* (Chicago: AMA, 1978).

13. Joseph P. Newhouse et al., "Some Interim Results from a Controlled Trial of Cost Sharing in Health Insurance," *The New England Journal of Medicine*, December 17, 1981, pp. 1501–1507.

14. Freeland and Schendler, "Health Spending in the 1980s."

15. Larry J. Freshnock, *Physician and Public Attitudes on Health Care Issues* (Chicago: AMA, 1984).

16. Christopher N. Theodore and Gerald E. Sutter, *Distribution of Physicians in the U.S., 1965* (Chicago: AMA, 1967); James N. Haug, Gene A. Roback, and Beverly C. Martin, *Distribution of Physicians in the United States, 1970* (Chicago: AMA, 1971); Louis J. Goodman, *Physician Distribution and Medical Licensure in the U.S., 1975*: Part 1 (Chicago: AMA, 1976); Catherine M. Bidese and Donald G. Danais, *Physician Characteristics and Distribution in the U.S.*, 1981 Edition (Chicago: AMA, 1982); Mary Ann Eiler, *Physician Characteristics and Distribution in the U.S.*, 1982, 1983 Editions, (Chicago: AMA, 1983); Gene Roback et al., *Physician Characteristics and Distribution in the U.S.*, 1984 Edition (Chicago: AMA, 1985).

17. Sharon R. Henderson et al., *Medical Groups in the U.S., 1980* (Chicago: AMA, 1982).

18. American Medical Association, "Number of Group Practices Rising in U.S." *American Medical News*, December 7, 1984, p. 17.

19. Roger A. Reynolds and Daniel J. Duann, eds., *1985 Socioeconomic Characteristics of Medical Practice* (Chicago: AMA, 1985).

20. Interstudy, *1984 HMO Census.*

21. Reynolds and Duann, eds., *1985 Socioeconomic Characteristics.*

22. Eiler, *Physician Characteristics.*

23. American Medical Association, "Physicians' Financial Arrangements with Hospitals," *SMS Report*, Volume 3, Number 6, September 1984.

24. Daniel J. Duann and Sara L. Thran, "Recent Changes in Medical Practice Characteristics," in Reynolds and Duann, eds., *1985 Socioeconomic Characteristics.*

25. Duann and Thran, "Recent Changes."

26. Duann and Thran, "Recent Changes."

27. Duann and Thran, "Recent Changes."

28. Proceedings of the AMA House of Delegates, Interim Meeting, 1983, (Chicago: AMA, 1983), p. 93.

29. N.T. Greenspon, "A Descriptive Analysis of Medical Malpractice Insurance Premiums, 1974–1977," *Health Care Financing Review* 1 (1979): 65–71.

30. National Association of Insurance Commissioners, "Executive Summary of the Medical Malpractice Closed Claims Study Conducted by the National Association of Insurance Commissioners," *Connecticut Medicine* 45 (1981): 91–101.

31. American Medical Association, *SMS Report,* Volume 4, March 1985, p. 37.

32. Proceedings of the AMA House of Delegates, Interim Meeting, 1985 (Chicago: AMA, in press).

33. Proceedings of the AMA House of Delegates, Annual Meeting, 1985 (Chicago: AMA, 1985), p. 113.

34. American Medical Association, *Health Manpower*, Board of Trustees Report C, Interim Meeting, House of Delegates, 1981.

35. American Medical Association, *The Effects of Market Forces on the Supply of Health Manpower*, Board of Trustees Report RR, Annual Meeting, House of Delegates, 1984.

TABLE 3.1
National Trends, 1982–1985, and Variation Across States, 1985

| | % Agree | | | | Difference |
	1982	1983	1984	1985	Across States
Doctors accessible	*	56	53	60	21
Fees reasonable	42	32	27	32	17
People are losing faith in doctors	62	66	68	64	18
Explain things well	55	49	44	50	19
Too interested in money	60	66	67	62	17
Doctors act like they're better than other people	33	35	38	42	14
Interested in patients	68	62	62	74	14
Poor able to get care	48	41	43	44	22
Up-to-date on medical technology	71	72	71	73	17
Elderly able to get care	52	50	45	52	22
Don't care	*	*	54	56	14
Medical science saves many	*	*	94	92	7
Lawyers fees reasonable	*	*	19	22	19
Become doctors to help people	*	*	51	65	22
Become doctors for money/prestige	*	*	66	61	21
Doctors spend enough time with patients	46	38	34	41	23
Suits justified	47	41	43	30	15
Limit on malpractice awards	61	62	61	56	19
Amount of money awarded, too much	47	45	41	44	24

TABLE 3.2
"Don't Know" Responses to Professional Liability (in percentage), 1982–1985

	1982	1983	1984	1985
Suits justified	10%	12%	13%	27%
Amount of awards	8	11	11	21
Limit on awards	4	3	5	13

TABLE 3.3
Number of U.S. Medical Schools, Graduates, Graduate Training Programs, and
Trainees, Selected Years, 1964–1986

Year	Medical Schools	Graduates	Graduate Programs	Interns/ Residents
1964-65	88	7,409	7,561*	41,568
1969-70	101	8,367	7,402*	51,015
1974-75	114	12,714	5,157*	NA
1979-80	126	15,135	4,816	65,936
1980-81	126	15,667	4,786	63,207
1981-82	126	15,985	4,743	69,738
1982-83	127	15,824	4,760	70,523
1983-84	127	16,327	4,759	72,397
1984-85	127	16,318	4,811**	75,125
1985-86	127	—	4,917**	74,514

Notes: *Includes freestanding internship programs.
**Increases from newly accredited pediatric subspecialty programs.

Source: Anne E. Crowley, et al., "Undergraduate Medical Education, *Journal of the American Medical Association* 246 (25 December 1981): 2913–2930, and 254 (27 September 1985): 1565–1572, 1585–1593; *Directory of Approved Internships and Residencies 1964, 1965, 1969* (Chicago: AMA, 1964, 1965, 1969); Anne E. Crowley, ed., *Directory of Residency Training Programs: 1983–1984, 1985–1986* (Chicago: AMA, 1983, 1985).

TABLE 3.4
FMGs in U.S. Graduate Medical Education, Selected Years, 1964–1986

Year	Total	U.S. Citizens	Aliens
1964-65	11,494	NA	NA
1969-70	16,307	NA	NA
1974-75	NA	NA	NA
1979-80	12,070	4,249	7,821
1980-81	12,078	4,790	7,288
1981-82	13,194	5,838	7,356
1982-83	13,123	6,388	6,735
1983-84	13,221	6,990	6,231
1984-85	13,525	7,386	6,139
1985-86	12,509	6,868	5,641

Note: NA = Data not available.

Source: Anne E. Crowley, ed., *Directory of Residency Training Programs: 1983–1984, 1985–1986* (Chicago: AMA, 1983, 1985).

TABLE 3.5
Number of FMGs Examined and Certified by ECFMG, Obtaining Initial License,
Selected Years, 1960–1984

Year	ECFMG Examinees	ECFMG Certificants*	FMG Initial Licensees**
1960	11,301	NA	1,419
1965	9,204	NA	1,528
1970	16,525	5,436	3,016
1975	20,415	6,542	5,965
1980	10,599	5,756	3,310
1981	13,212	7,063	3,131
1982	13,759	6,731	4,196
1983	13,365	7,127	4,753
1984	15,602***	7,634	4,094

Notes: *"Certificants" includes persons taking VQE as well as persons taking
ECFMG (or FMGEMS in 1984). Not all certificants apply for a license in the
United States.
**Licensure information by citizenship not available.
***"1984 Examinee" count includes number taking FMGEMS in July 1984.

Sources: Anne E. Crowley, ed., *Directory of Residency Training Programs:
1985–1986* (Chicago: American Medical Association (AMA), 1985); and AMA,
Department of Medical Education Information Analysis, unpublished data.

TABLE 3.6
ECFMG Examinees and Certificants by Citizenship, Selected Years, 1960–1984

Year	USFMGs		FNFMGs	
	ECFMG Examinees	ECFMG Certificants	ECFMG Examinees	ECFMG Certificants
1960	NA	NA	NA	NA
1965	NA	NA	NA	NA
1970	824	250	15,701	5,186
1975	2,157	215	18,258	6,327
1980	4,070	655	6,529	5,101
1981	5,180	1,127	8,032	5,936
1982	6,047	1,304	7,712	5,427
1983	7,311	1,442	6,054	5,685
1984	6,222	1,524	9,380	6,110

Note: NA = Data not available.

Sources: AMA, Department of Medical Education Information Analysis,
unpublished data; and Educational Commission on Foreign Medical Graduates,
selected annual reports, 1970–1985.

TABLE 3.7
FMGs Participating in MATCH, Entering Residency Programs, Selected Years, 1960–1986

Year	Participants in MATCH	Successfully Matched	PGY-1 Residents	Total Residents
1960	82	71	1,753	9,935
1965	NA	NA	2,361	13,829
1970	470	244	3,339	19,613
1975	3,074	1,056	2,784*	16,037
1980	1,143	645	NA	12,078
1981	1,663	872	NA	13,194
1982	3,335	1,287	NA	13,123
1983	4,923	1,593	2,901	13,221
1984	5,907	1,674	3,045	13,525
1985	5,948	1,589	2,672	12,509
1986	4,965	1,382		

Notes: NA = Data not available.
  *End of internship, beginning of flexible programs.

Sources: Educational Commission on Foreign Medical Graduates, selected annual reports, 1970–1985; and National Resident Matching Program, selected annual reports, 1970–1985.

TABLE 3.8
USFMGs Participating in MATCH, Entering Residency Programs, 1980–1986

Year	Participants in MATCH	Successfully Matched	GPGY-1 Residents	Total Residents
1980	NA	NA	NA	4,790
1981	536	362	NA	5,838
1982	943	536	NA	6,388
1983	1,305	644	1,778	6,990
1984	1,695	752	2,846	7,386
1985	1,692	671	1,569	6,868
1986	1,303	503		

Notes: NA = Data not available.

Sources: Educational Commission on Foreign Medical Graduates, selected annual reports, 1970–1985; and National Resident Matching Program, selected annual reports, 1970–1985.

TABLE 3.9
Foreign National FMGs Participating in MATCH, Entering Residency Programs,
1980–1986

Year	Participants in MATCH	Successfully Matched	PGY-1 Residents	Total Residents
1980	1,143	645	NA	7,288
1981	1,127	510	NA	7,356
1982	2,392	751	NA	6,735
1983	3,618	949	1,123	6,231
1984	4,212	922	1,199	6,139
1985	4,256	918	1,103	5,641
1986	3,662	879		

Note: NA = Data not available.

Sources: Educational Commission on Foreign Medical Graduates, selected annual reports, 1970–1985; and National Resident Matching Program, selected annual reports, 1970–1985.

TABLE 3.10
Number and Percentage of FMG Physicians and Active Physicians Who Are FMGs, Selected Years, 1970–1983

Year	Number FMGs	% of MDs Who Are FMGs	Number Active FMGs	FMG as % Active MDs
1970	57,217	17.1%	55,396	17.8%
1975	80,848	20.5%	78,717	21.5%
1980	97,726	20.9%	94,995	21.8%
1981	102,762	21.2%	98,972	22.2%
1982	107,284	21.4%	103,232	22.3%
1983	112,005	21.6%	107,590	22.4%

Sources: AMA, Department of Medical Education Information Analysis, unpublished data; Annette Van Veen Daigle, ed., *U.S. Medical Licensure Statistics, 1982, 1983* (Chicago: AMA, 1984, 1985); and AMA, division of Survey and Data Resources, unpublished data.

TABLE 3.11
Number of Active and Inactive Physicians in the United States, Selected Years,
1965–1983

	1965	1970	1975	1980	1981	1982	1983
Active	277,575	311,203	366,425	435,545	444,899	462,947	479,440
Inactive	13,279	19,621	21,449	25,744	35,011	35,690	36,911
No information	1,234	3,204	5,868	6,390	5,213	3,321	3,195
Total	292,088	334,028	393,742	467,679	485,123	501,958	519,546

TABLE 3.12
Number of Active Physicians in Patient Care, Selected Years, 1965–1983

	1965	1970	1975	1980	1981	1982	1983
Patient care	259,418	278,535	311,937	376,512	389,369	408,663	423,361
Other prof. activity	18,157	32,310	28,343	38,404	41,376	40,726	43,436
Not classified*		358	26,145	20,629	14,154	13,558	12,643
Total active	277,575	311,203	366,425	435,545	444,899	462,947	479,440

Note: *Not classified category established in 1970.

TABLE 3.13
Number of Active Physicians by Major Professional Activity, Selected Years, 1965–1983

	1965	1970	1975	1980	1981	1982	1983
PATIENT CARE	259,418	278,535	311,937	376,512	389,369	408,663	423,361
Office-based	185,338	192,439	215,429	272,000	288,038	299,191	309,891
General practice	65,744	52,023	47,015	48,020	49,947	51,007	51,932
Medical specialties	38,110	44,428	54,876	76,090	82,019	86,717	90,098
Surgical specialties	53,964	59,271	67,501	81,931	86,056	88,643	91,177
Other specialties	27,520	36,717	46,037	65,959	70,016	72,824	76,684
Hospital-based	74,080	86,096	96,508	104,512	101,331	109,472	113,470
Physicians in training*	43,506	51,228	57,802	62,042	63,349	68,986	73,171
Full-time staff	30,574	34,868	38,706	42,470	37,982	40,486	40,299
OTHER PROFESSIONAL ACTIVITY	18,157	32,310	28,343	38,404	41,376	40,726	43,436
Medical teaching	9,794	5,588	6,445	7,942	7,202	7,505	7,783
Administration	4,057	12,158	11,161	12,209	13,250	13,408	13,828
Research	4,306	11,929	7,944	15,377	17,901	16,743	18,535
Other	—	2,635	2,793	2,876	3,023	3,070	3,290
ACTIVITY UNCLASSIFIED**		358	26,145	20,629	14,154	13,558	12,643

Notes: *Includes interns, residents, and fellows.
**Not classified category established in 1970.

TABLE 3.14

Average Physician Net Income After Expenses, Before Taxes, 1984

All physicians	$108,400
Specialty	
General/family practice	$ 71,100
Internal medicine	103,200
Surgery	151,800
Pediatrics	74,500
Obstetrics/gynecology	116,200
Radiology	139,800
Psychiatry	85,500
Anesthesiology	145,400
Census division	
New England	$ 87,300
Middle Atlantic	98,400
East North Central	109,400
West North Central	110,700
South Atlantic	114,500
East South Central	122,200
West South Central	119,100
Mountain	102,300
Pacific	109,400

TABLE 3.15
Mean Fee for an Office Visit with an Established Patient, 1974, 1979, 1984*

	1974	1979	1984**
All physicians	$10.95	$17.17	$26.09
Specialty			
General/family practice	$ 8.75	$13.67	$20.71
Internal medicine	12.28	19.89	29.89
Surgery	11.27	17.61	25.65
Pediatrics	10.38	15.65	24.11
Obstetrics/gynecology	13.10	19.04	31.16
Census division			
New England	$11.71	$17.60	$27.72
Middle Atlantic	12.60	18.57	29.48
East North Central	9.99	15.46	23.13
West North Central	9.50	13.55	21.26
South Atlantic	11.05	17.54	25.17
East South Central	9.24	15.24	21.49
West South Central	10.17	16.26	25.77
Mountain	9.83	16.35	23.80
Pacific	11.55	19.53	30.98
Type of practice			
Solo	$10.82	$17.23	$25.83
Non-solo	11.13	17.09	26.38
Location			
Nonmetropolitan	$ 8.05	$13.47	$19.16
Metropolitan			
Less than 1,000,000	10.19	15.65	24.63
1,000,000 & over	12.38	19.50	29.54
Physician age			
Less than 36	$10.94	$16.94	$26.19
36–45	11.28	17.16	26.99
46–55	10.90	17.62	26.03
56–65	10.85	17.15	25.59
66 or more	10.56	16.54	24.18

Notes: *Data are based on information from physicians in all specialties
excluding psychiatry, radiology, anesthesiology, and pathology.
  **Caution should be observed in comparing 1984 results with previous
years because of changes in methodology made in the transition from the
periodic surveys of physicians to the socioeconomic monitoring system.

Sources: AMA, Socioeconomic Monitoring System Surveys, 1982–84; and AMA,
Periodic Surveys of Physicians, 1975–80. The population from which samples
are drawn includes only active nonfederal patient care physicians, excluding
residents.

TABLE 3.16
Average Total Professional Expenses of Self-Employed Physicians, 1984

	Average Expenses
All physicians*	$ 92,600
Specialty	
General/family practice	$ 89,000
Internal medicine	89,500
Surgery	131,200
Pediatrics	78,200
Obstetrics/gynecology	119,400
Census division	
New England	$ 65,100
Middle Atlantic	82,500
East North Central	83,000
West North Central	99,700
South Atlantic	98,100
East South Central	99,800
West South Central	116,300
Mountain	85,500
Pacific	98,100

Notes: *Includes physicians in specialties not listed separately.

TABLE 3.17
Type of Contract for Physicians with Direct Payment Arrangements with Hospitals by Sex, Experience, Net Income*

	Salary	Fee for Service	% of Net Dept. Billing	% of Gross Dept. Billing	Other
All physicians	60.4%	41.1%	7.5%	11.8%	24.2%
Sex					
Male	59.3	42.9	8.1	12.8	25.3
Female	70.3	26.7	2.7	4.1	15.1
Experience					
0–9	62.7	40.8	8.5	11.7	22.9
10–19	58.3	45.2	7.1	12.9	25.0
20–29	60.5	37.1	5.1	9.9	26.8
30 or more	56.3	39.7	9.2	13.2	24.4
Net income (in 000s)					
0–49	71.8	39.3	4.8	4.8	17.9
50–74	77.7	33.6	8.1	11.8	22.2
75–99	63.7	32.1	5.9	9.7	16.9
100–149	49.6	45.6	6.7	11.0	38.2
150–199	42.0	60.8	10.0	26.0	21.6
200 and over	35.5	45.2	16.1	19.4	38.7

Notes: *Net income is defined as income after expenses but before taxes. The percentages reported in the table exceed 100 percent because some physicians have more than one financial arrangement.

TABLE 3.18
Annual Claims per 100 Physicians

	Annual Claims per 100 Physicians	
	1980–1984	Prior to 1980
All physicians	8.6	3.0
Specialty		
General/family practice	7.4	2.9
Medical specialties	5.7	2.4
Surgical specialties	13.9	4.4
Region		
Northeast	10.7	3.1
North Central	8.2	2.6
South	7.3	2.6
West	8.9	3.7

Source: AMA Socioeconomic Monitoring System survey, 4th quarter, 1984.

4

The Future of the Medical Profession

Rosemary A. Stevens

The long-term future of the American medical profession may now be playing out, quietly but insistently, in the choices made by undergraduates in deciding whether or not to apply to medical school. Just as applications to dental schools have fallen rapidly in the last decade, applications to medical schools may decrease dramatically in the next ten years. In all probability, the fashion for a medical education—the enormous popularity of the medical profession as a career that distinguished the years from the mid-1940s to the mid-1980s—is on the wane: victim of the high costs of education, of an oversupply of physicians, and of society's willingness to control physician numbers, incomes, and behavior.

Everywhere there are signs of constriction on traditional professional prerogatives: in high malpractice insurance rates, derived from huge settlements in the courts which reflect, in turn, a reservoir of public skepticism about the standards and motives of medical professionals; in the frenetic growth of health care organizations, in which physicians are subordinate to highly paid executives; in the willingness of government to force change on medical practice and medical education through Medicare and Medicaid; in the growth of consumer self-help groups; and in the lay and business leadership of major disease intervention programs for alcoholism, stress reduction, counseling, and weight control. The physician's role seems, somehow, diminished. It is easy to sketch a scenario of a profession in decline; to express concern about the quality, socioeconomic mix, evolving attitudes, and motivations of students entering the pipeline in the 1980s; and to foresee a generation of disaffected medical cynics, carrying large debts and unfulfilled expectations.

However, as in most of life, the picture is more complicated, ambivalent, contingency-ridden, and subject to unexpected changes than any simple scenario can suggest. There is not one future for the medical profession but a kaleidoscope of possible developments. Even simple generalizations are difficult to make. For example, the accepted notion of professional dominance—the physician's autonomy in making clinical decisions, controlling medical resources, and practicing as (and where) he or she thinks fit—is clearly weakened in the 1980s.[1] Nevertheless, although the profession may lose power in one area, it may gain power in another. Thus it is not enough to talk about the declining authority of the medical profession without substantial qualification, including increased opportunities for physicians to become managers and negotiators within health care systems.

The theme of this chapter is that we are moving, awkwardly, but profoundly and permanently, toward new definitions of the "medical profession" and "professionalism" in the late twentieth century; toward fundamental shifts in assumptions; and toward rearticulated roles for professional organizations. Indeed, what is exciting about the next twenty years is the growing need—indeed the demand—for a new frame of reference in which to assess contemporary changes. The professional snake is shedding its skin.

From the prospect of the late-1980s, the metamorphosis—the clean lines of the new order—is impossible to predict but there are hints, apparent in the pressures now being imposed upon professional behavior and roles, in the sociocultural environment of medicine, and in physicians' reactions to them. Here, I shall focus on three broad areas of change: (1) the trend toward organized and supervised practice of physicians; (2) the appearance of the articulate patient, in roles as diverse as a purchaser, a consumer of care, and a partner in medical treatment decisions; (3) challenges to the underlying cognitive and structural bases of medicine, as symbolized in the structure of medical specialties and in the educational milieu in which doctors are trained.

I do not intend to duplicate the detailed analysis of changes in different areas that form the substance of the other chapters. Rather, I seek to find patterns across these disparate areas that suggest specific changes in medicine as a profession. I will then return to the more general questions subsumed in my charge. What are the most likely futures for the medical profession and its institutions? How is the profession to view itself? And how will it be viewed? Since medicine has numerous possible futures, depending on decisions and events across an interdependent matrix of variables, it makes little sense to describe changes in a single, straightforward narrative. Thus, I will list my specific, illustrative observations as if each were, indeed, a cell within a larger matrix.

Supervised and Corporate Practice

1. Physicians in the 1980s are rushing toward practice in organizations: group medical practices, health maintenance organizations (HMOs), preferred provider organizations (PPOs), managed health care systems. Although opinions vary as to how much of the population will be served by HMOs within ten years (probably 20–40 percent of the population), most other individuals will also be served by physicians working in organized practice arrangements, including group practice and independent practice associations. Between 1980 and 1984 alone, there was a 44 percent increase in the number of identified group practices in the United States.[2]

The movement of physicians to organized arrangements will continue, pressured by the growth of organized payment arrangements (HMOs, PPOs) which require physician practice organizations of some sort; by the double economic whammy of declining visits to physician offices and hospitals and competition from an increasing pool of physicians; and by the convenience and emerging convention of a corporate environment as the appropriate place for practice. There is little future for physicians outside of practice systems, except perhaps on the fringes of medicine or in highly specialized activities. New definitions of the medical "profession," including codes of professional ethics, have to assume that the average physician's work and behavior are conditioned by organized, bureaucratic workplace arrangements.

2. The successful medical practice organization in the United States is business-oriented and highly sensitive to external organizational, economic, and political environments. A former president of the American Group Practice Association recently told an audience of group practice physicians that "your success in the future will depend upon your ability to raise capital, the strength of your management, and your ability to do good, competent marketing. Growth will be a part of that capitalization and your ability to develop and market new services."[3] Traditional discussions within medicine, articulated most clearly in the 1930s, assumed that the notion of a "profession" is separate from and antagonistic to that of "commerce"; the former is altruistic, the latter is driven purely by self-interest. This rhetoric has been useful in defining medicine as a profession with at least some public responsibilities, even though private, fee-for-service practice has long distinguished physicians as the proprietors of small service businesses. Present-day trends toward overt commercial practices within medicine demand an adjustment of

the rhetoric, at least. Since the old rhetoric suggested that commerce corrupts ideals, it is important for professional organizations to articulate appropriate patterns of professional behavior which are free from the old dichotomous beliefs; in short, to replace or reinvent the rhetoric in terms which reflect today's practice pressures. If the notion of professionalism is to survive, it needs a new primer of etiquette. What are the acceptable and unacceptable modes of behavior that distinguish the term "professional" in the late twentieth century?

3. The trend toward more comprehensive patient care within organizations parallels a potentially widespread move to pay for physician services by capitation. Administration calls for capitation payments through Medicare,[4] if implemented, will have as profound an effect on physician practice patterns as DRGs have on hospital care. Notably, multi-specialist group practice will be encouraged and perhaps become the norm; physician groups or networks will have a direct incentive to evaluate the distribution of costs and resources across the specialty fields encompassed in the services they offer collectively; and the capitation fee system will provide a vehicle for external monitoring of performance and a need to justify practice-specific behavior by physicians. Under Medicare capitation, congressional committees would need to assure themselves that patients were not being shortchanged or given inferior care. Subscribers would benefit from information on comparative services given by different groups for the same capitation fee. Moreover, in a system dominated by organized groups, all physician groups in an area would have a collective interest in presenting a combined front to Medicare agencies or their agents in renegotiating the capitation fee. Thus, professional skills will increasingly require negotiating and public relations skills by the practice corporations as a whole and an awareness of individual physician behavior and external incentives and controls by physicians within the groups. Resistance to external regulation will, in the long run, be self-defeating.

4. Medical group practices traditionally have not developed tight self-policing mechanisms over their own physicians.[5] However, peer review organizations as well as major hospitals have begun to monitor physician behavior in terms of costs and benefits, identifying the relative profitability of individual practice patterns to the institutions, and designating individual physicians as money-raisers or money-losers. For example, the University Hospital of Cleveland was featured in a recent cover story of a major health management journal for its "manufacturing style management organization similar to those used in automobile plants,"[6] based on productivity. General managers are expected to step in if a physician orders too many tests and to keep watch on physicians who attract a large number of lawsuits.

One organizational model for the future is balanced confrontation; that is, sharper physician/hospital or physician/health system conflicts, pitting managers against both individual physicians and physician organizations. However, hospitals have their own problems and they no longer form the single, natural, organizational center of the health care system. A more interesting possibility is the development of coalitions of interest between health care organizations and medical groups, with each side responsible for its own sphere of operations, held in tension by mutually reinforcing goals: the survival and prosperity of a health care system, challenged from without by competing systems, payer groups, and public and private regulation. This model requires the development of well-run physician practices (corporations) which are able to develop organizational policies and exert management authority over their physician members. It remains to be seen whether the medical profession will be able to see the benefits of self-organization and self-policing in corporate units—either as freestanding units with negotiated relationships with independent health care corporations, or as subsidiary units of health care systems.

5. I do not see the future health care system dominated by a few huge national corporations. Perhaps no more than 35 percent of all hospitals will be part of chains by 1990.[7] However, at the local level, e.g., within a city, it seems increasingly likely that health care will be carved up among a relatively small number of organized systems, some of which will be part of larger chains. As the physician marketplace becomes, in effect, a closed system of competing units, the doctor's professional allegiance will be to a health care organization. The role of local medical societies may become either less or more important: less, if corporations meet physicians' needs; more, in climates of general physician dissatisfaction.

6. The physician of the future will be able to practice because he/she holds a "job." The job will be sought by advertisement, a recruitment firm, or the use of formal and informal networks (such as referral of residents by trusted evaluators in specific teaching programs). The individual will be recruited through competition. Significantly, he/she will be assessed not only on technical and behavioral skills but on conformance to the prevailing corporate "style," corporate goals, and corporate ethos. Medical students and medical residents will need to be sophisticated readers of the job market and be aware of divergent corporate expectations.

7. Supervised medical practice by external agencies will continue: through government (through peer review organizations and other mechanisms), through health care organizations (via management information systems and other controlling mechanisms), through other insurance

intermediaries, and through fourth parties, notably employers. Employers
are already intervening in physician decision-making through requirements for hospital utilization reviews and second surgical opinions. In
one study of 1,185 companies in 1984, 40 percent reported that they
required retrospective hospital utilization review, 34 percent required
concurrent review, 25 percent required preadmission review, and 28
percent mandated a second surgical opinion.[8]

Large physician groups may be able to counter some of the supervision
and control by providing alternative self-policing mechanisms. Indeed,
in the long run, attempts by outside agencies to establish detailed practice
norms (and to enforce them) may become both economically meaningless
and functionally self-defeating. Regulation assumes that practice can be
standardized—hence DRGs. However, medicine is not infinitely reducible
to standards of measurement. Indeed, in many chronic diseases we may
see increased variety in practice style in different settings, rather than
increased conformity. Where responsible physician organizations are
recognized, regulation over practice may be delegated to these in the
future—provided such organizations are in place—leaving, as external
controls, cost limits and patient satisfaction measures. Large-scale organizations may thus imply a wider collective responsibility by professional groups for professional standards in the future.

8. Supervised and corporate practice represents a significant and
lasting change in the American medical profession, bringing both problems and opportunities in its wake. It is easier to see the problems
than the opportunities because: supervised and organized practice represents a shift in the traditional professional doctrines of American
medicine, which have long emphasized individual autonomy in practice
and distrust of the "corporate practice of medicine"; the shifts have
been engineered by forces external to the medical profession, thus
threatening the control of medicine by its own national professional
organizations; and perhaps of most significance, these shifts coincide
with other major challenges to medicine in the late twentieth century,
creating a combined sense of powerlessness, onslaught, and doom within
the medical profession. Such challenges include the increasing physician
supply and changes in the formal social regulation of professions as
trades, including the role of the Federal Trade Commission and anti-
trust regulation.[9]

Even more central to the future role of the medical profession are
the overlapping changes in the behavioral and cognitive aspects of
medicine, suggested in the next two sections; that is, in the doctor-
patient relationship, and in the structure and meaning of medicine.
These combined pressures mask the opportunities inherent in changing

organizational forms; opportunities, that is, both for individual and for collective professional authority.

Public Distrust and Patient Power

9. The basic tenets of the medical profession have come under increasing criticism in the past decade inside, as well as outside, the medical profession. Medicine's most venerable icon, the Hippocratic Oath, is openly criticized at medical meetings in the 1980s as inappropriate and outdated: for example, by giving paternalistic power to physicians over patients, by excluding a social role for physicians, and by implying that interventionist treatment is always better than doing nothing.[10]

10. Concerns about physician incompetence and the ability of the profession to police itself—at least, as yet—are commonplace. Medical licensing boards are criticized as understaffed and as tending to work in isolation from each other. Fraudulent medical credentials are often accepted; hospital medical staffs have been reluctant to inform upon physicians known to be of inferior competence, even dangerous; most disciplinary actions, when they do exist, have not been publicized, and there continues to be enormous variation in the rate of disciplinary actions from state to state.[11]

The phenomena themselves are not new. What is new is public interest and awareness through television reporting and the press, and acknowledgment by professional organizations that self-policing does not work effectively through the traditional licensing and credentialling system. There is much breast-beating.

Rather than blame the failures on the licensing boards, it may be better to ask how physician competence can be assured, in the future, within organized practice systems. Moreover, it should be observed that the licensing boards, as basic mechanisms of professional control, were developed in the late nineteenth and early twentieth century to create a strong, unified profession—and that they were very successful in achieving this goal. They are not necessarily appropriate to medicine in the late twentieth century. Thus, the criticism itself is perhaps misdirected.

11. Physicians are also criticized for not fulfilling patient expectations; that is, for failing to deliver on the promise of technological and scientific "progress" that was the main message of the reform of the medical profession at the beginning of the century (the so-called Flexner reforms) and was carried further by formal specialization between the two world wars. The promise was to advance medicine as applied science. Yet ironically, in its most dramatic applications this movement, too, is

questioned. The heralded era of organ transplantation from the mid-1950s, the increased technical potential of artificial organs and body parts, and the ability to sustain life on machines—each representing dramatic technological developments in medicine—have also emphasized the limitations of technology in improving the quality of life, and hence the limitations of physicians. For example, widespread use of kidney dialysis—and the boast that the United States, unlike more "rationed" countries, makes this technique available to all in need—has been joined by a growing awareness of problems in the clinical area, including side effects, and in the moral and psychological spheres of patient care.[12] The definition of good medical care has gone far beyond the scientific and technical. Yet, at the same time, the physician has lost much of his/her mystique. The future physician is neither fully scientist nor shaman. The new role model (or myth) does not yet exist. It will.

12. The obvious difficulty in reconciling the heroic status of artificial heart transplant teams with the strokes and sufferings of the supposed beneficiaries has been managed, in part, by making the patient part of the treatment team. Thus the recipient, too, becomes a kind of hero. Indeed, the artificial heart recipient may be seen as an emblem of a wider set of shifts, in which the patient gains power vis-à-vis the physician; that is, where the old doctor-patient role of superior and dependent, or expert and passive recipient of expertise, is replaced by a doctor-client or partnership arrangement. The patient, in short, becomes an active participant in jointly made decisions.

The end of the era of the passive patient is most noticeable in decisions affecting the terminally ill. Such decisions have moved, in large part, from the private, informal domain of physician decision to the negotiated or bureaucratic domain. Physicians have been indicted for murder in cases where life-sustaining equipment was withdrawn from a comatose patient, even where family approval was assumed. Patients' wishes about life or death may be codified in "living wills." Indeed, the very definitions of life and death, originally the exclusive province of physicians, have become a matter for legal guidelines and national debate.[13]

13. If patients are seen as consumers as well as partners in the healing process, a major shift in power relationships between the public and the profession can be observed. Insuring organizations have become agents of consumers rather than of providers, able to exert control through the power of the pocketbook. At the same time, the increased role of nonphysicians in areas of great importance to health maintenance has challenged the central role of physicians in the medical arena. Much of the work now being done in the United States to control obesity, alcoholism, anorexia, stress, and individual behavior is being done under

the aegis of lay organizations such as Weight Watchers or through the health programs of major business corporations. Moreover, much of this work has been defined as education and behavior modification rather than as "medicine."

The cumulative impact of the increased role of patients in clinical decision-making, of public criticism of medical organizations and of medicine itself, and of developments of health services outside medicine, could suggest a more limited role for the medical profession in the future. However, these changes can be seen, equally, as part of the larger readjustments in medicine. Direct comparison of the present with the recent past is less important—certainly less fruitful—than reassessment of the full range of physician activities in the present.

Physicians appear to have accepted, even to have welcomed, the new emphasis on the role of the patient in decision-making and the patient's right to refuse treatment. However, there is also concern lest the pendulum sway too far in the other direction: toward abdication of responsibility by physicians, unsound medical judgment by patients, and unwilling collusion by physicians and patients, leading to decisions against the patient's own better judgment.[14] This tension reflects the (as yet) uncompleted shift to a new kind of medicine that seeks to involve the patient through adequate understanding of the patient's approach to life, health, and to disease, through a doctor-patient encounter that explores the psychodynamics of the illness in each and every specific case. How can physicians, collectively, manage a positive readjustment of their role to allow for major changes in doctor-patient relationships? What are the incentives and opportunities for the profession that are inherent in this change?

14. In terms of previous attitudes and ideologies of medical practice, the emphasis on "talking medicine" has three profound—indeed revolutionary—implications. First, it puts psychosocial skills and joint planning at the forefront of the medical encounter, forcing the physician to think of health and disease in terms of subjectively defined notions like suffering, hope, and pain, rather than in terms purely, or even predominantly, of the external, concrete evidence of disease. Various attempts to define the approach and skills necessary to undertake this complex task have been grouped under calls for a new "humanism" in medicine.[15]

Second, this type of encounter takes time: to talk, to listen, and where necessary to educate and to persuade—thus potentially lengthening the physician encounter at a time when fees are being controlled and shorter encounters appear more "cost-effective." Third, it assumes a potentially wide variability in the nature of individual treatment decisions, rather than the repetition of standard treatment measures in all cases that present similar "medical" symptoms.

15. The new humanism thus runs counter to pressures imposed on physicians via Medicare reimbursement. Indeed, there is a worrying dissonance between perceptions of medical practice which suggest increasing variation in individual patient care, based on effective patient-physician encounters, and a reimbursement system based on standardization and reproducibility across medical care incidents. Not only do DRGs assume the systematization of medicine around standard forms of practice, but interest in small-area variations in practice patterns assumes that there is, somewhere, some arbitrary, if not ideal mean for defined categories of care. Excessive standardization of medical practice through the reimbursement system will lead to profound moral questions about individual patient care and individual (patient) freedom of choice of care. One major task for the medical profession is to map and justify the type, range, and nature of practice in the era of the "active patient," and suggest how it should be assessed and monitored—and by whom.

16. Just as the notion of the patient's role is shifting from the legitimated dependency of the "sick role" to more active involvement in clinical decision-making, physicians are seeking to develop roles and skills that allow for complexity and uncertainty, rather than assuming that scientific expertise lays down "one best way" of proceeding in most cases. In turn, redrawing the doctor-patient relationship implies new definitions of medicine, diagnosis, and disease. The medical profession has ridden triumphantly through most of the twentieth century along a road paved with assumptions and structures about disease that are based on the infectious diseases. Today's major medical problems encompass chronic diseases—conditions which are often long-term and messy, and are not usually susceptible to a single diagnosis, intervention, and cure. Neither doctors nor patients have yet developed an appropriate set of behavior or an ethos for a medicine based on chronic disease. These are major activities for the future.

Medicine and Its Institutions

17. As Anselm Strauss and others have pointed out, there is a curious inappropriateness in today's prevalence of chronic illness amid the profession's images and practices of acute care. In hospitals, personnel still tend to think of themselves as treating patients who are acutely ill and of cure as the only successful outcome of disease. Nevertheless, the work of physicians, nurses, and technicians has been radically altered by the prevalence of chronic illness and the technologies to manage such diseases. Chronic disease patients, playing an active rather than a

passive role in the management of a chronic condition, also engage in substantial work in the course of the illness. The patient's role in hooking up and monitoring kidney dialysis equipment is a notable case. The increased diffusion of technology from hospitals to patients' homes also involves patients in active work with machines. However, the patients' own effort, or work, has usually been ignored in the hospitals where most nurses and physicians are trained.[16] The two sets of perceptions are potentially (and dangerously) at cross-purposes.

18. The shift from an infectious to a chronic disease mode of thinking within the profession—and from a single diagnosis to a complex of problems—is not new; it has been developing for at least fifty years. The effect is cumulative and can no longer be ignored.

19. Major professional institutions are out-of-date in both their structure and assumptions. There is an acknowledged gap between medical education and major health problems such as asthma, arthritis, or chemical dependence.[17] There have been few studies of the effect of health care programs on individual health. Indeed, the general lack of outcome measures for chronic diseases—and a serious lack of interest in outcome studies—has created a major gap in knowledge about the relative effects of different forms of medical intervention on patients' health and well-being.[18] Clinical studies performed in health facilities may have little relevance for assessing the health status of the majority of individuals in any one year who are sick outside of institutions. There are few measures of the effectivenesss of home care. Of perhaps most importance, the professional "culture" of medical schools has given little importance to such questions—at least, as yet.

20. The infectious disease era was based squarely on medical research. Identifying bacteria and viruses in the laboratory was translated, at least in theory, into scientific interventions—"magic bullets"—against specific diseases. In contrast, research on chronic diseases is enormously varied, drawing on a wide range of biomedical and applied sciences, focused on underlying biological mechanisms. Basic research into disease mechanisms and processes, which may have long-term payoffs in understanding and treating diseases such as cancer, is undertaken in large part by research specialists who are not physicians. Epidemiological research on chronic diseases is a peripheral activity in most medical schools. The odd position has been reached where American medicine is distinguished, in part, by its emphasis on research and technological development, but medicine as a profession in the late twentieth century lacks a discrete, focused, formal body of knowledge for application in the field.

21. In the early years of the twentieth century, the reform of the American medical profession, with medical education based on uni-

versities, was justified by centering medical education around research—in laboratories and on the hospital wards. The second major professional movement, the growth of specialization, was predicated on technological advances in research and practice. In an era of chronic disease, the medical profession cannot define itself and its institutions so sharply around scientific research and/or technology, as they are presently understood. A new defining focus is needed. What this will be is not yet clear.

22. Marked differences of medical opinion about treatment have appeared in recent years, in cases ranging from breast cancer to coronary bypass surgery. A current example is the debate on whether psychosocial variables can affect the course of cancer. Different research draws diverse conclusions about the relationship between the patient's emotional state and the outcome of disease.[19]

Such debates, however invigorating and good for the advancement of medical knowledge, have important structural effects. First, they further weaken the traditional authority of the physician as the "expert with the answer"—a matter of concern only if one believes that this traditional authority should be maintained. Second, such debates lead to the involvement of the patient in discussions of alternative forms of care and relative risks. Indeed, they require that the patient be sufficiently sophisticated to understand that physicians may have an individual style of practice and beliefs about particular diseases. One physician may be more interventionist than another; a second lean towards surgical intervention; a third toward chemotherapy; a fourth favor psychotherapy; and so on.

There is, in short, a climate of medical uncertainty, for both patients and physicians.

23. In this environment of uncertainty and risk, doctor and patient are, ideally, bonded as allies, working jointly to achieve the optimal effect. It follows that they may need mutual reassurance that each did all they could, when medical intervention fails to arrest the course of disease. For example, a recent contribution to the *New England Journal of Medicine* urged physicians to be present at the patient's funeral.[20] By doing so, the physician may reassure family members and help with their guilt after a patient's death, and demonstrate his/her caring about the patient as an individual, particularly when the last days have been dominated by machines. In turn, the funeral provides the physician with a ritualized "ending" to a course of treatment in which there were no single or obvious decisions. The typical physician has not been trained to cope with notions of disease that transcend his/her actual "medical attendance," nor to share any sense of defeat with patients or their relatives. The opportunity here is for the physician to become

more "human" and, perhaps, more trusted as an individual. The fear is lack of authority and lack of distance. Enormous psychological shifts are required of individual physicians, during this period of transition, at a time when morale is already low. Such an observation suggests aggressive efforts by professional, corporate, and other groups to encourage or establish discussion and intervention programs, designed to develop perceptual change.

24. The structures of medical education still largely follow the pattern set up at the time of the Flexner Report (1910), designed to streamline and standardize medical curricula to produce a well-trained medical journeyman, educated in the basic and clinical sciences within a university setting. Graduate medical education (residency training in the specialties) follows the patterns set up in the 1920s and 1930s: training based on acute care in hospitals, within subdivisions of medicine or "specialties," based on technologies, diseases, organs, systems, or age groups. Neither pattern of education is ideally designed for, or easily adjustable to today's practice, which applies a wide range of technologies to a wide range of chronic diseases.

Both undergraduate and graduate medical education are therefore under stress. Medical school curricula are criticized in blue-ribbon reports for requiring the memorization of facts, rather than the acquisition of skills, values and attitudes, and the development of knowledge through self-critical, independent learning.[21] Meanwhile, under the onslaught of numerous crosscutting specialized fields, the structure of specialty certification is becoming complicated and unwieldy. There are now twenty-four medical specialties, with forty-two subspecialty areas. However, many of these new areas are attempts to reinvent generalized practice or to link established technologies across traditional specialties. For example, both internal medicine and family practice have an interest in geriatric medicine, while six specialties (anesthesiology, internal medicine, obstetrics and gynecology, pediatrics, psychiatry and neurology, and surgery) have endorsed a subfield of critical care.

Continuing appraisal of medical education by professional groups is expected in the next decade, culminating (perhaps) in major changes. Possibilities for change include new national specifications about undergraduate education, enforced through accreditation, external funding, or consensus; more flexible specialty board requirements; alternative forms of specialist education offered by universities and/or health care systems, outside the board system. One possibility is for major service organizations to train their own physicians at the graduate level, or to contract for training in different fields with selected universities. In any event, the large health care systems (via their medical groups or otherwise) will have an increasing voice in specifying the nature of the specialties.

25. External influences on academic health centers and on the financing of graduate medical education, even in the 1980s, attenuate the traditional authority of medical organizations to dictate the form and structure of professional education. Notably, the reform of medical schools in the early twentieth century was accomplished under the strong medical leadership of the Council on Medical Education of the American Medical Association, in a climate of public compliance and/or approval. Likewise, the specialty boards were generated from preexisting specialist associations and interests within medicine. The present crisis in medical education forms a major, third phase of professional development in the twentieth century. In this phase, the game will be played by different rules, in which the power of professional organizations has to be justified and negotiated anew. Strong, effective leaders could build confidence within the profession and create confidence in the profession from outside. Weak or disorganized leadership may lead to a steady erosion of professional self-governance and prestige.

26. Changes affecting the medical profession are easiest to see where they take place in the external political arena rather than within; for example, in debates over reimbursement policy, physician supply, or the number of residencies. It is also easiest for any group to rally its forces to cope with outside threats, rather than to rethink its basic assumptions and its internal order. Nevertheless, the assumptions built up in the old era of educational reform and infectious diseases conflict, in numerous ways, with the demands of consumerism, cost-control, and chronic disease. The educational system has produced an abundance of physicians practicing in the subspecialties; relatively few with knowledge ranging over the technology of home care, the management of large physician organizations, and the development of comprehensive services, including social services for long-term care. Hospitals may no longer be the best or only place to train all specialists. Yet, inertia in the system has inhibited major change. How the institutions of medicine will change in response to the rapidly changing environment is still, alas, unclear.

27. Fundamental assumptions built into professional priorities and ranking systems demand re-examination. For example, the assumption that a specialty field is defined, in large part, by its claim to technique or to a focused body of research breaks down in fields such as family practice and general internal medicine: fields which define themselves functionally—as managers or gatekeepers of comprehensive care. Nevertheless, a national study of heads of departments of medicine, reporting in 1985, criticized programs in general internal medicine for their inability to conform to the focused research programs and NIH funding that distinguish other nonsurgical specialties. Development of a research program in general internal medicine was said to be the most significant

reported problem in the field, as perceived by the departmental chairman.[22] However, there was no specification as to what this research might be, and no discussion of the possible value of a field whose research interests might be wide-ranging, across a variety of disciplines—or even, of a field with relatively little focus on scientific investigation. Research has become a Pavlovian reflex.

There are, in short, changes both in the external environment and within the profession of medicine. These changes are interlinked. They include pressures on both the structures, and underlying ideology and assumptions of the profession. The future success of the medical profession rides on the ability of its leaders and organizations to manage change in both the external and internal spheres.

The Medical Profession: Possible Futures

One possible future for the medical profession is to hold on to the old ideas and assumptions of medical authority, developed through the earlier successful periods of medical reform (1890–1917) and of specialization (1920–1970), and to resist further changes for as long as feasible. But this stance is self-defeating. Indeed, the American medical profession is already embarked, willy-nilly, upon a new period of major change.

For students of the professions, the present period is of enormous intellectual interest. I expect a flowering of good sociological analysis of concepts such as professional dominance and authority, the patient's role, the doctor-patient relationship, and the social construction of disease. The very nature of a "profession" is under reappraisal. Such a prospect may seem a hollow comfort to physicians struggling with the impact of present-day changes. Nevertheless, I think that a better understanding of the magnitude and multifactorial character of present shifts will allow the profession to escape the dangers of unthinking opposition. The opportunities need also to be created.

In earlier periods of professional change in the twentieth century, professional leaders and groups developed new, even radical institutions and movements, based on clearly stated missions: upgrade the medical schools, control standards in surgery, provide an orderly subdivision of medicine into specialties. Today, there is ambivalence about the appropriate role of a profession at all—ambivalence which calls for clearer statements by those major organizations. Otherwise, action will be frozen.

Charles Bosk recently reviewed assumptions about professions in terms of two competing traditions in sociology,[23] and these serve well here. First, there is the "classical myth": that the professions are essentially different from other occupations, that they deserve a high degree of autonomy in the workplace, and that they can be trusted by society to operate in the public interest through a rigorous code of ethics and through governance by their own associations. Second, there is the "anti-myth": that professions are merely devices created out of the self-interest of an occupational group, in order to further its goals in the marketplace. Hence, in Bosk's phrase, discussions of the profession oscillate between idealism and cynicism, depending on the author's point of view. Arnold Relman's plea for a "return" to a medical profession infused by idealism and moral principle is the clearest example of the tendency to choose one of these views.[24] By choosing the "myth" as a basis for argument, physicians can be seen as swept into a period of commerce and greed, and as losing some of the attributes that make them a "profession." Alternatively, all medical actions can be couched as self-serving exercises of power, a jockeying of interests in which rhetoric services economic interest. Both these points of view are useful. Alone, neither is an ideal mind-set for viewing the present, complex picture of professional change in medicine, with a view to prediction or prescription.

I think that we are now in a remarkably exciting, fluid period, which may last for many years, of constant debate, negotiations, organizational and ideological adjustments, out of which a new consensus about the nature of the medical profession will emerge. It is too soon to see what this consensus will be. However, it is fruitless to see present changes as having only deleterious effects upon the profession. The future profession may well be different, but it may be equally powerful and equally successful. The key is the ability to shift from outmoded expectations and perceptions.

Perceptual shifts are difficult, in part, because the potential pluses and minuses of professional change do not always fall within the same category of analysis. Thus, an apparent economic or organizational constriction might have unexpected cognitive or clinical benefits—or vice versa. Even among the changes I have sketched out here—and many others could be delineated—positive elements of change have to be set against the more obvious negatives. For example, for individual physicians, practice in large-scale medical organizations may be much more interesting and relevant to clinical work, in an era of chronic illness, than practice in a relatively narrow specialty setting. The identification, within the corporate setting, of a large group of patients also provides the element of what the British call a "practice," i.e., the opportunity for a group of physicians to accept collective responsibility for a community of care and to review the progress of patients through their careers of health and disease. Large organizations also centralize information systems, providing physicians with a potentially better means of self-examination, clinical and epidemiological research than is available to government through PROs, or to organized payers.

The fee-for-service private practice system has long made physicians mini-business executives. Translation to an organized setting may make such skills more sophisticated, specialized, and useful. At the same time, organized systems may allow for increased physician-participation in resource allocation across the spectrum of medical care, and perhaps for the exercise of more clinical initiative within the sheltering arms of a corporation, than in more exposed forms of practice. Large corporations can also extend their grasp much more readily than small group practices to encompass social services, home care, and other necessary adjunct services for the effective management of chronic disease.

Positive as well as negative outcomes can also be suggested in other areas. In the future, physicians will undoubtedly earn less, in real terms, than they have in the period of enormous physician incomes in the past forty years. However, they may also have more time to spend with patients—a necessary aspect of doctor-patient cooperation—and they may also find that practice is more intellectually engaging and satisfying as a result. The number of malpractice suits might even decline in number. Debates within medicine about the nature of disease, appropriate forms of treatment, and the role of patient attitudes and behavior promise a fertile, open, exciting arena for debate about fundamental questions within medicine. We do not yet know what the various results will be. My point is that change is not necessarily all in one direction.

The development of the medical profession in the late twentieth century may be seen by future historians as the third major period of professional change in the twentieth century—at least as important as the changes that led to a reformed medical educational system by 1917 (and to a national medical profession), and to a structure for specialization by World War II. Today, as in the earlier periods, basic ideas about medicine demand as much attention as the structure of professional organizations, controls, and incentives. How far—and how—the organizations of medicine will respond to the complex changes in medicine's environment remains to be seen. Meanwhile, the system itself is implementing change—just as it did at earlier periods of professional reform.

If professional organizations and individuals see today's changes as necessary, manageable, and negotiable, and as having potentially positive effects, the present generation of medical students may feel privileged to be entering medicine, despite its various uncertainties—and the profession may have a stronger voice in its own destiny. Medical schools may become more varied in the future than they have in the past: the structure of specialty certification may become a less controlling system: the role of practitioners within physician organizations may produce new forms of practice. All such developments—and others—carry with them the opportunity for creating a new, more appropriate, more interesting profession.

Notes

1. See Eliot Freidson, *Professional Dominance: The Social Structure of Medical Care* (New York: Harper and Row, 1970); and Paul Starr, *The Social Transformation of American Medicine* (New York: Basic Books, 1983).

2. Carol Brierly Golin, "Remodeling the House of Medicine," *American Medical News*, 17 May 1985.

3. David J. Ottensmeyer, President of the Lovelace Medical Foundation, cited in Golin, "Remodeling the House."

4. "Changes Sought in Doctors' Pay Under Medicare," *New York Times*, 7 December 1985, 1–8.

5. See Eliot Freidson, *Doctoring Together* (New York: Elsevier, 1975).

6. Kathy A. Fackelman, "Cleveland Hospital on the Road to Product-Line Management," *Modern HealthCare*, 22 November 1985, pp. 70–77.

7. Editorial, "Hospital Chain Expansion Over?" *Modern HealthCare*, 22 November 1985, p. 5.

8. Hewitt Associates, "Comparing Practices in Health Care Cost Management, 1984," reported by Jeff Charles Goldsmith in Eli Ginzberg, ed., *The U.S. Health Care System: A Look to the 1990s* (Totowa, N.J.: Rowman & Allanheld, 1985), p. 53.

9. See e.g. Clark C. Havighurst, "Doctors and Hospitals: An Antitrust Perspective on Traditional Relationships," *Duke Law Journal* (1984): 1071–1162; Leigh C. Dolin, "Antitrust Law Versus Peer Review," *New England Journal of Medicine* 313 (1985): 1156–57.

10. e.g. Thomas Swick, "At ACP Session, an Ancient Code is Scrutinized," *American College of Physicians Observer*, December 1984, pp. 20, 22.

11. e.g. a CBS *60-Minutes* program featuring fraudulent credentials, September 1, 1985, and a series of articles on physician incompetence in the *New York Times*, 2–3 September 1985.

12. See Renee C. Fox, Judith P. Swazey, and Elizabeth M. Cameron, "Social and Ethical Problems in the Treatment of End-Stage Renal Disease Patients," in Robert O. Narins, ed., *Controversies in Nephrology and Hypertension* (New York: Churchill Livingstone, 1984), pp. 45–70.

13. President's Commission for the Study of Ethical Problems in Medicine and Biomedical and Behavioral Research, *Deciding to Forego Life-Sustaining Treatment* (Washington, D.C.: GPO, 1983); and Barbara Mishkin, "Decisions Concerning the Terminally Ill: How to Protect Patients, Staff and the Hospital," *HealthSpan*, the Report of Health Business and Law, 2 (March 1985): 17–21.

14. Peter M. Marzuk, "The Right Kind of Paternalism," *New England Journal of Medicine* 313 (1985): 1474–76.

15. See e.g. Richard Gorlin and Howard Zucker, "Physicians' Reactions to Patients: A Key to Teaching Humanistic Medicine," *New England Journal of Medicine* 308 (1983): 1959–63; and American Board of Internal Medicine, "A Guide to Awareness and Evaluation of Humanistic Qualities in the Internist," June 1985.

16. Anselm Strauss, et al., *Social Organization of Medical Work* (Chicago: University of Chicago Press, 1985).

17. For example, see D. Shine and P. Demas, "Knowledge of Medical Students, Residents, and Attending Physicians about Opiate Abuse," *Journal of Medical Education* 59 (1984): 501–7; Health and Public Policy Committee, American College of Physicians, "Chemical Dependence," *Annals of Internal Medicine* 102 (1985): 405–8.

18. Barbara Starfield, "Motherhood and Apple Pie: The Effectiveness of Medical Care for Children," Milbank Memorial Fund Quarterly/*Health and Society* 63 (1985): 523–46.

19. B.R. Cassileth et al., "Psychosocial Correlates of Survival in Advanced Malignant Disease?" *New England Journal of Medicine* 312 (1985): 1551–5 and correspondence, ibid. 313 (1985): 1354–59; "Strong Emotional Response to Disease May Bolster Patient's Immune System," *New York Times*, 22 October 1985, C-1.

20. Patrick Irvine, "The Attending at the Funeral," *New England Journal of Medicine* 312 (1985): 1704–5.

21. A notable recent example is "Physicians for the Twenty-First Century," *Journal of Medical Education* 59 (1984), Part 2.

22. Robert H. Friedman and Janet T. Pozen, "The Academic Viability of General Internal Medicine," *Annals of Internal Medicine* 103 (1985): 439–44.

23. Charles L. Bosk, "Social Controls and Physicians: The Oscillation of Cynicism and Idealism in Sociological Theory," in Judith P. Swazey and Stephen R. Scher, eds., *Social Controls and the Medical Profession* (Boston: Oelgeschlager, Gunn and Hann, 1985), pp. 31–51.

24. Arnold S. Relman, "The New Medical-Industrial Complex," *New England Journal of Medicine* 303 (1980): 963–70.

5

Employment of Physicians at Harvard Community Health Plan

Stephen C. Schoenbaum

In contrast to the other chapters which consider broad sectors of the American medical community, this chapter is devoted to a close case-study examination of the physician employment practices in a single health maintenance organization (HMO). Harvard Community Health Plan (HCHP) which began operations in 1969 with eighty-eight members, by January 1986 had become a 210,000-member HMO with nine health centers located around the Boston area (Figures 5.1 and 5.2). It is not a typical HMO since it started with a special relationship to Harvard University and some of its teaching hospitals. Nevertheless, as HCHP has grown over the past seventeen years, it has confronted and continues to confront issues of changing medical practice and changing physician personnel which may be instructive for others in a variety of health care settings.

Background

HCHP is a staff model HMO. As such, its physician staff are salaried employees and there is a single line relationship which can be drawn from the president (CEO) to the medical director (COO) down to the level of each physician's practice. This structure differs from the group model HMO in which the group of clinicians who care for HMO members is organized separately from the entity which enrolls the members; and generally the group practice receives a capitation (a certain number of dollars per member per month) for providing services to HMO members. The structure of HCHP also differs from that of an independent practice association (IPA), which is currently the most rapidly growing HMO model. In an IPA, the entity which enrolls the members contracts with independent practitioners to provide care to its members. The mode of reimbursement to the independent practitioners could be a capitation. More commonly it is a percentage of usual charges for the services rendered, with the remainder held in escrow for distribution if the total expenditures of the HMO are less than its revenues.

The basic operating unit at HCHP is the health center. The oldest and largest center has 54,000 members. Other mature centers are smaller and have 20,000 to 40,000 members. New health centers usually begin with a few thousand members, many of whom have transferred from an older center when the new one is closer to the home or workplace. Each health center, regardless of size, contains at least four departments with center-based chiefs: internal medicine, pediatrics, obstetrics/ gynecology, and mental health. In addition, medical and surgical specialty services are provided physically within each center, but they are organized on a plan-wide basis. Thus, there are central departments of surgery, orthopedics, visual services, neurology, oncology, cardiology, etc., and each such department has a central chief.

Nurse practitioners and other nonphysician health professionals have long played an important role in the delivery of health services at HCHP. In its early years HCHP employed nurses. Then, as the desire grew to incorporate nurse practitioners into the delivery of primary care, HCHP undertook a major training program to develop its own group of nurse practitioners. These practitioners have been used universally in the internal medicine departments where one practitioner has worked with one or two physicians. HCHP is currently adopting a model of internal medicine practice in which there will be a fixed ratio of one nurse practitioner to each two full-time physician equivalents. Thus, it is important to keep in mind as we discuss physicians' practices that these physicians are working not alone but rather in a team arrangement with nurse practitioners.

Development of Physician Staffing at HCHP

At its inception there was one health center, the Kenmore Center, and HCHP physicians were recruited from the staffs of Harvard teaching hospitals, primarily the Beth Israel Hospital and the Peter Brigham Hospital. The latter is now a division of Brigham and Women's Hospital (BWH). As HCHP became solvent, physicians were no longer paid through their initial hospital affiliation, and they became direct salaried employees of HCHP. Nevertheless, the relationship to the teaching hospitals remained strong, and HCHP's adult patients were admitted to them. Though many physicians were full-time at HCHP, particularly in the departments of internal medicine, pediatrics, and obstetrics/

gynecology, some part-time physicians were hired from the outset. The part-time physicians in primary care departments tended to divide their work between HCHP and a function in an affiliated teaching hospital or possibly with home responsibilities. They did not have private practices outside the plan. In mental health, part-time physicians and psychologists have been the rule; and most of these part-time staff have split their professional activities between HCHP and private practice. The nature of mental health practice inside and outside HCHP differs: Within the HMO, psychiatrists have placed a strong emphasis on care of psychotic patients and others with serious mental health problems, while their private practices have been weighted towards patients with problems of living or adjustment. Some have argued that to concentrate on one or the other type of practice would be professionally confining or possibly too much of an emotional strain. Thus, the model of part-time staffing in this field has persisted.

For a different reason, staffing in the surgical departments also began with part-time employees. This pattern was needed in order to have enough individuals in the department to provide on-call coverage twenty-four hours a day, seven days a week and to cover subspecialties within the department. Thus, for example, with approximately one full-time surgeon for every 22,000 members, it would take a moderately large staff model HMO to support a full-time surgical staff of four members. In contrast, a rather small HMO could support three or four quarter-time surgeons.

HCHP's relationship to the Harvard teaching hospitals was atypical, indeed unique, for an HMO. Only recently have other HMO arrangements begun to develop from academic departments. The relationship was useful for HCHP recruitment in several ways: in internal medicine HCHP has had an active residency and fellowship training program which has provided potential recruits with an opportunity to have a genuine practice experience at HCHP and, in turn, has provided HCHP chiefs an opportunity to evaluate potential recruits firsthand. In departments such as surgery, it has been possible for the plan to take advantage of the high quality of recruits in the teaching-hospital-based departments and provide a general practice outlet for the staffs of those departments. In parallel, there have been advantages for the academic departments and their chairmen: HCHP has been a convenient location for placing trainees with an interest in practice. In addition, the availability of HCHP as a practice location and the accompanying solid funding for clinical physicians has permitted academic department chairmen to expand their departments with researchers or to develop subspecialists without the need to provide full salaries. It is likely that this has allowed some academic departments to grow at a faster rate than otherwise would have occurred.

HCHP's second center opened in Cambridge, Massachusetts in 1973. The founding members of this center were two academic physicians on the staff of Cambridge Hospital, a city hospital which is also a Harvard teaching hospital. The staff in primary care fields was largely, though not exclusively, recruited from Harvard training programs. The center's staff in the specialties was recruited from the staff of Cambridge Hospital. Most of these physicians were not full-time members of the academic department at Cambridge Hospital but were practitioners associated with the hospital. Not all of the recruits were salaried employees. Some of the specialty physicians developed a contractual relationship with HCHP (a subject which will be expanded below). In other respects, however, the physician staffing pattern resembled that of the Kenmore Center, the principal difference being the teaching hospital with which the staff was affiliated.

Planning for a third center began in the mid-1970s. It was originally envisioned that this center, to be located in Wellesley, Massachusetts, would have a relationship with an outstanding community hospital in that area, the Newton-Wellesley Hospital, and that the relationship would be similar to that of the Cambridge Center and Cambridge Hospital or the Kenmore Center and the in-town teaching hospitals. The physician staff of the Newton-Wellesley Hospital, however, most of whom were in private fee-for-service practice, strongly opposed an affiliation of the hospital and HCHP. Indeed, one byplay of this was that several of the local practitioners who were Harvard Medical School alumni and who were incensed by HCHP's move into their area began a campaign through the Harvard alumni association against HCHP's use of "The Harvard Name."[1] At this time, HCHP recognized that it could not depend on local hospitals for affiliation of its centers, and since it wanted a more appropriate institution than the tertiary teaching hospitals for hospitalization of patients with secondary care needs, it purchased a small hospital in Boston which is now called HCHP hospital.

The fact that the Wellesley Center, located approximately ten miles from downtown Boston, could not affiliate with the nearest hospital, led to several changes within HCHP. Though it would have been possible to staff the primary care departments with full-time and part-time center-based personnel, it would have been essential to staff the specialty departments from Boston, and, as it turned out, largely from the Kenmore Center. This led to the clear recognition that HCHP did not consist of a confederation of separate centers, like McDonald's franchises, but instead was a multi-center system of care. It was at this time that the central departments of surgery and orthopedics were established, and chiefs were appointed with plan-wide responsibility. It is important to keep in mind the fact that staffing or recruiting was really the central problem addressed by the central departments. In an organization predominantly managed within an operating unit, i.e., health center, it took an important problem, specialty staffing, to precipitate the development of a separate management structure which cut across operating units—the central clinical services.

Recently another staffing problem has arisen requiring a different solution. In July 1984, HCHP opened its sixth health center, located in Peabody, Massachusetts, eighteen miles from downtown Boston. Until that time, HCHP centers had been located close enough to Boston so that while some of the residents in the area around the center used local hospitals, many used hospitals in Boston. Thus, HCHP's pattern of using hospitals in Boston was not alien to many, perhaps most, of its suburban members. The population of the North Shore area in which the Peabody Center was located, however, rarely used Boston hospitals. Therefore, it would not have been possible to build the center without an affiliation with a local hospital. Furthermore, since none of the local hospitals was a teaching hospital, it was necessary to work out contractual arrangements for specialty coverage with existing community groups of physicians who used the hospital with which the affiliation arrangement was established. These requirements led to complicated multilateral negotiations which eventuated in a series of contracts with the Beverly Hospital and with several groups of practitioners on its staff.

Effects of Growth on Recruitment

HCHP has been growing steadily at 15–20 percent per year throughout its history. While growth has provided opportunities to expand staff and particularly to expand the skills provided inside the organization, it has also posed interesting problems in physician recruitment.

In early 1981, after over a decade of its existence, HCHP enrolled its 100,000th member, and in mid–1985, it enrolled its 200,000th member. Though the growth rate had not changed, a difference in recruiting practices was needed to provide sufficient staff for the enlarged membership. To understand this, it is necessary to examine staffing ratios, such as the ones in effect at HCHP (Table 5.1). For example, if the staffing pattern in an HMO is one full-time equivalent orthopedist for every 20,000 members, then for 20,000 total members four quarter-time orthopedists would be required to provide appropriate on-call coverage. As the HMO grew to 40,000 members, probably a several year process, new orthopedists would be added or the four existing orthopedists would increase their practice to half-time, which would eliminate the need for new recruits. At HCHP, until there were 100,000 members, specialty departments grew largely by a combination of adding new part-time physicians and by increased time commitments from existing staff. At about that size, with a 20 percent annual growth rate, a new type of problem presented itself. It became apparent that within a one- year period there would be a sufficient number of new members to require the addition of a full-time equivalent orthopedist, and that in subsequent years, assuming continued growth, progressively more full- time equivalents would be needed. There were several difficulties in filling this need with additional part-time physicians, and we shall examine this problem below.

Even in the primary care departments, continued growth at HCHP has placed a great strain on the traditional recruiting mechanisms: Beyond 100,000 members, growth required hiring more internists and pediatricians each year, numbers large enough to outstrip the capability of Harvard teaching programs to serve as the predominant recruitment pool. Thus the chance to become familiar with potential recruits by working with them during their training has been diminished, as has the importance of the "old boy network" which permitted plan chiefs to request references on potential recruits from friends and colleagues on the Harvard faculty. It also has become necessary to formalize the recruiting mechanisms in most departments. In 1984, the first director of physician recruitment was appointed. A physician-manager, his functions have included development of recruitment marketing techniques so that HCHP can attract appropriate numbers and types of candidates who are qualified to be on the staff of the plan and its affiliated hospitals. He has also played an important role in the increasingly difficult problem of placing new physicians in mutually optimal locations: Different centers do not just have a need for new internists or gynecologists. They may have a particular demand for female physicians or for older physicians, for physicians who are experienced at handling the problems of inner-city children, or for physicians who are willing to have a primary care practice but also have an interest in a subspecialty such as endocrinology, etc.

A specific example of some of the changes that have occurred in HCHP's physician staffing arrangements with growth and of the opportunities and problems indicated above, is HCHP's Department of Orthopedics: As the hypothetical example above suggests, in the early days of HCHP, when there were few members, all of the orthopedists were part-time. Almost all were members of BWH's Department of Orthopedics, a highly specialized department with an international reputation. The general pattern was that newly hired orthopedists at BWH would work part-time at HCHP. This allowed the chairman of the BWH department to add talented budding academic orthopedists to his staff without having to support them entirely from research funds or BWH's practice base. The two departments grew together well for over ten years. Along the way one full-time orthopedic surgeon was hired by HCHP, and he was affiliated with the smaller academic Department of Orthopedics at the Beth Israel Hospital. In general, the staffing ratio was one full-time equivalent orthopedist per 20,000 members. At about the time HCHP had 100,000 members, several problems occurred. First, the BWH department had reached a large size and was neither willing nor able to continue growing to meet HCHP's manpower needs. Second, most of the part-time HCHP orthopedists who were on the staff of BWH were unwilling to increase their time commitment to HCHP. Indeed, about this time several of them had established strong reputations in specialty areas of orthopedics and realized that they could support themselves at least as well, and at the same time further their academic specialty careers, if they did not undertake orthopedic work at HCHP. Third, HCHP's chief of orthopedics was one of the part-time BWH-affiliated physicians and was caught between his two bosses and their needs: HCHP's need to continue to staff its growth and the BWH department's need to limit its growth and limit competition for precious operating room time. Consequently, over the next two years several of the part-time orthopedists left HCHP to concentrate their activities at BWH, while HCHP appointed its only full-time orthopedist as its department chief, mounted a major recruiting effort which led to the hiring of several new full-time orthopedists plus some new part-time orthopedists, entered into a contractual relationship with a non-academically affiliated practicing group of orthopedists to provide services to members in one of the centers most distant from the teaching hospitals, and equipped HCHP Hospital to handle all but the most complicated orthopedic cases.

Employment Arrangements with Physicians

HMOs can be thought of as having many "make-versus-buy" decisions which determine the services which will be supplied in-house and which services it will obtain elsewhere. For example, all HMOs must provide cardiac surgery and neurosurgery to their members when their medical conditions warrant these services; but only the very largest HMOs have cardiac surgeons or neurosurgeons on their staffs. The most common alternatives to direct employment of physicians include contractual relationships with individual physicians or groups of physicians for specified amounts of patient care (e.g., three office sessions a week plus a share of the on-call rotation) or for specified types of care (e.g., all professional services related to performance of a heart transplant), or simply the purchase of care on a fee-for-service basis as needed.

At HCHP most physician services are provided by salaried employees. For many years explicit or implicit work expectations in return for salary were defined by department chiefs. Recently, plan-wide explicit work expectations have been defined for the major clinical departments. Work expectations in HMOs are usually defined either by the amount of time the physician is expected to work (e.g., a full-time internist will spend "x" hours seeing ambulatory patients in office sessions, perform the hospital care associated with those patients, and have a full share of the on-call schedule) or by establishing the size of the panel of patients for whose care the physician is responsible (e.g., a full-time internist working with a half-time nurse practitioner will provide all ambulatory medical care for a panel of "xx" members, perform the hospital care associated with the panel, and have a full share of the one-call schedule). HCHP, in going to plan-wide work expectations, has adopted panel-size based expectations for the primary care departments. The definition of panel-size is complicated and will depend at a minimum on the age distribution of the membership of the HMO, since an internist cannot care for as many older adults as young ones and a pediatrician cannot care for as many young infants as older children.

Similarly, there are many ways to set up compensation systems. At HCHP, as at a number of older HMOs, for many years all salaries were indexed to one specialty, and within a specialty the distinctions in salary between physicians related solely to years of prior experience in medicine and years of service at HCHP. Performance distinctions between physicians were not expressed in salary distinctions. Thus, at HCHP the salary scale for internists had a ranking of 1.0, and other specialties had scales which were a fixed multiple of the internal medicine salaries; i.e., psychiatry was 1.14, surgery was 1.22, orthopedics 1.55, etc. There was a 70 percent difference between the highest and lowest salaries within a scale; and it took eight years of experience within the plan (now six) to traverse the scale within a specialty if one's prior medical experience was limited enough to necessitate starting at the lowest rung of the salary ladder. Currently at HCHP, as at many other HMOs, incentives are being built into the physician compensation system. Furthermore, specialties are no longer indexed to each other. Rather, the scale for each specialty is now determined in part from a "marketplace" assessment of earnings in that specialty.

To develop an incentive compensation, it has been necessary to develop a more formal physician review process. At HCHP, new physicians have always had two reviews, one at nine months and another at two years, before they obtained permanent employee status. Now, physicians who have worked five years or more at HCHP are being reviewed every year by their chiefs of service. Areas which are covered in the review include the quality of care provided, with attention to technical knowledge and skills, interpersonal and service skills, and the physician's role as leader of the care team (the nurse practitioner and clinical assistant). The review also covers practice management skills, cost-effectiveness of practice style, participation in nonclinical activities in the plan, continuing education, and participation in teaching or research. The review is written by the chief and is submitted to the medical director.

Contractual arrangements with physicians are common in many HMOs. There are a number of reasons why the HMO or the physician might want a contractual relationship rather than a salaried employee status. For instance, a physician who is being recruited to work for the HMO part-time and is already in fee-for-service practice may find the usual salaried arrangement undesirable because he or she already has a professional corporation, does not need the HMO's fringe benefit arrangements, and would be more attracted to the HMO position if the benefits could be converted to cash (a problem which may be solved only by a contract). This can be generalized to any situation in which a potential recruit who is highly desirable from the HMO's standpoint finds the standard employment arrangement disadvantageous. An example of a situation in which the HMO prefers a contractual relationship is the situation in which an HMO usually salaries physicians to provide a fixed fraction of a full-time equivalent position but now wants to hire a group of physicians to care for its growing membership in a capitation arrangement.This would necessitate a contract, but would provide the HMO with exactly as much care as its membership needs. Thus the HMO would not hire a full-time surgeon-equivalent in anticipation of rapid growth when a half-time surgeon-equivalent would be sufficient. A contract would enable the HMO to demand the coverage equivalent of a full-time surgeon when the membership warrants it, but would pay for only a part-time surgeon at lower membership.

Of course, both advantages and disadvantages accrue to each party in a contract as well as in a straight employment arrangement. Contracts generally contain provisions for cancellation without cause, whereas in many HMOs physician employees have the equivalent of tenure and can be terminated only for cause. Contractors are unlikely to feel the same loyalty to the organization as do employees. Also, an HMO inclined to frequent contracting to get around its own employment conditions is unlikely to be able to maintain the morale of its employees. In short, it is essential to weigh the advantages and disadvantages of contracting, and it is desirable to have policies indicating sanctioned uses of contracts.

In the world of fee-for-service medical practice, there has been a simple elegance to the monetary incentive system. By and large, physicians who perform services technically well, in volume, or in a way that is satisfying to patients, have been rewarded monetarily. There are some inequities: some technically skilled physicians who are not nice to their patients make a fortune, while some highly personally satisfying physicians who spend inordinate amounts of time with their patients earn relatively little. On the whole, however, physicians tend to be rewarded for what they do, and if patients do not like the treatment they receive from one physician, they can change to another.

Devising a suitable reward system has proved to be a difficult task for HMOs since there are many different types of behavior an HMO may wish to reward. An HMO wants members to receive appropriate medical care, but it also wants to ensure that physicians do not overutilize resources such as laboratory tests, consultations, hospitalization, and procedures. Only recently has this become a concern in the fee-for-service world. In addition, the HMO must demand that physicians are accessible to members and provide personally satisfying care during encounters since members often do not have many, if any, alternatives to the clinicians they are seeing, and members are contracted to stay with the HMO for up to one year before a switch to another care system is possible. Unfortunately, while there are several good reasons for HMOs to encourage these patterns of behavior, there has been no simple or generally accepted incentive. In a newly opened center, HCHP has attempted to address this problem by establishing a new compensation system. While physicians will receive a "draw salary," which will be 85 percent of the standard HCHP scale, an annual performance fund has also been established. This fund is generated from achievement of targeted objectives for average panel size, patient satisfaction levels, out-of-office and hospital utilization costs, and quality of care indicators. The distribution of the performance fund to individuals is determined on the basis of a merit review conducted jointly by the chief and department members and can amount to as much as 25 percent of the draw salary during the performance period.

Alternatives to Physicians

To provide care to its members, HCHP employs a variety of professionals in addition to physicians. These include nurse practitioners, physicians' assistants, nurses, psychologists, social workers, physical therapists, nutritionists, optometrists, and podiatrists. In mid-1985, HCHP employed 271 full-time physicians about one-half of whom were primary care internists or pediatricians. At the same time, HCHP had

185 mid-level clinicians, predominantly nurse practitioners and physicians' assistants.

It is axiomatic that as an HMO grows in size and in the complexity of the services which it makes rather than buys, it will include additional types of health professionals. It is only slightly less obvious that once an HMO has employed a nonphysician health professional, almost invariably at lesser cost, it becomes possible to consider substitution of physician services for those of the nonphysician. Nurse practitioners have been effective in providing care in ambulatory practice settings,[2] and it has already been mentioned that they are embedded in the provision of care in the primary care departments at HCHP. Many work in other departments as well, such as urgent care or triage. Until recently, physicians' assistants have been employed primarily in surgical specialty areas and urgent care, but now they are being hired in primary care departments as well. Member satisfaction with the services provided by these nurse practitioners and physicians' assistants is high, indeed similar to satisfaction with physicians. Clearly, it has been possible for physicians to extend the care that they give to members by working closely with a nurse practitioner or physicians' assistant.

Another example of the use of nonphysicians is HCHP's use of a podiatrist. Routine podiatry is not a benefit provided to HCHP members, except for those members with diabetes mellitus or peripheral vascular disease. Until a few years ago, HCHP contracted with a podiatrist to provide only those covered services. In the reorganization of the orthopedic department described above, it was apparent that it would be dificult to recruit sufficient numbers of orthopedists and that it would be desirable to use substitutes for orthopedists when possible. Many consultations with orthopedists were for foot problems which fit nicely within the range of skills of podiatrists. Accordingly, HCHP obtained additional services from a podiatrist so that the department of orthopedics could allocate some orthopedic referrals to the podiatrist. This substitution has functioned effectively for HCHP and its members, although routine podiatric care is still not a covered benefit.

There are some health professionals who provide substantively different types of care from those rendered by physicians, sometimes for problems similar to those treated by physicians. Chiropractic and acupuncture are examples of these. Neither is a covered benefit for HCHP members. HMOs do differ in their approaches to these types of care. For example, at least one HMO in the Boston area does offer chiropractic services to its members. The general issue involved here is the definition of the benefit package to which members subscribe. There is no real controversy about the value of routine podiatry or routine dental care, but many HMOs, probably most, do not offer them routinely. Were the HMOs to offer these services, it would require an increase in premium and a potential loss of competitiveness against less comprehensive, less expensive packages, or alternatively, curtailment of other types of services in order to keep the premium down.

Effects of Growth on Organization of Services

HCHP's growth from 100,000 to 200,000 members has been accompanied by a number of changes within the organization. As mentioned earlier, this growth involved a structural change from two centers which provided care independently to their memberships to a multi-center system of health care. Specialty services such as oncology and cardiology, which began with part-time physicians or with physicians who split their time between primary care and specialty care, have developed into freestanding units. Services which once were bought are now provided in part or wholly within the HMO. These include audiology, physical and occupational therapy, fundus photography, diagnostic ultrasound, mammography, exercise testing, electroencephalography, GI endoscopy, and vascular surgery. In order to bring most of these services in-house, it has been necessary to develop central management structures and to hire specialized allied health personnel and specialized physicians.

Interestingly, as HCHP has grown, it has decentralized its laboratory services. Laboratories in each health center now perform over 70 percent of the tests ordered by clinicians in those centers. When the plan was smaller, there was a single central laboratory to perform routine testing; only phlebotomy was done within the health center. The central laboratory has been dissolved and tests which cannot be done within the ordering health center are handled either by another center or by an outside vendor. In contrast, cytology and anatomic pathology, which once were performed by outside vendors, are now in-house services.

There is no hard-and-fast rule about which services should be brought in-house and which should remain outside. It is a fluid process which requires periodic reassessment of the cost-effectiveness of the current arrangement, coupled with an assessment of whether there is managerial capability for handling an alternative. It is usually easier to bring a service in-house than to disband an in-house service in favor of an outside vendor, since the latter generally requires reassigning or laying off employees and decisions about capital equipment which has been in use.

Many types of services still are purchased at HCHP. To name a few: CT scanning and nuclear medicine (for which we have contracts favorable enough to forestall bringing the services in-house), angiography, neurosurgery, cardiac surgery, and plastic surgery. Hospital services, which have been both performed and bought by HCHP, are likely to be bought to a greater degree in the future. Recent changes in the hospital industry are leading to a greater availability of beds at a time when the needs of growing HMOs, such as HCHP, are increasing. Since even a large HMO has a bed requirement which would fill only a small hospital (approximately one bed per thousand members per day), it is likely that many HMOs will make alliances with existing hospitals rather than create new ones. HCHP has developed a long-term contractual relationship with BWH, in which BWH will become the principal hospital site for most of HCHP's centers near Boston. An emergency service for HCHP members is being built at BWH. Over the next several years, a highly interdependent relationship is expected to develop. One consequence of the new arrangement has been the closing of HCHP Hospital, another demonstration of the fluidity of the make-versus-buy decision.

Changing Location of Care Delivery

It has been apparent for many years that HMO members have lower rates of hospitalization than patients in fee-for-service practices, and a Rand study[3] has demonstrated that this is the result of fundamental differences in practice, not as a result of skimming the healthiest members of the population or skimping on necessary care. The fundamental differences are multiple. They are likely to include more judicious selection of patients for hospitalization and the specific substitution of ambulatory services for inpatient services. In many HMOs, such as HCHP, where most ambulatory care is delivered within a health center, it is possible to perform tests, procedures, and give treatments that formerly were given in the hospital; and the tendency is to design units that increasingly permit this substitution. For example, HCHP recently built a central oncology unit which includes a day treatment center. In this unit, it is possible to administer forms of chemotherapy which heretofore were given only to hospitalized patients.

While the Rand study did not demonstrate clearly that length of stay (LOS) was lower for patients who were hospitalized by physicians in an HMO than for patients in fee-for-service practices, it is likely that some HMOs have adopted practices which would decrease LOS and that others have led their communities in devising programs to decrease LOS. The improving technologies associated with home care are likely to prove as appealing to HMOs as to those under the pressure of DRGs. At HCHP, the use of home care services has been stimulated by development of the Outside Health Resources Utilization Program in which skilled nurse practitioners make daily rounds to HCHP's hospitalized patients and evaluate early in a hospitalization what kinds of arrangements would facilitate discharge from the hospital or transfer to a more appropriate institutional setting. HCHP has contracted with a single large home health agency not only to achieve a volume discount but also to manage smoothly the interface between the patient at home and the physician in the office. Many of the efforts of the Outside Health Resources Utilization Program have been directed toward educating clinicians about home health care, since most physicians did not learn much about home care in their training; and for those who did, that knowledge is becoming rapidly outmoded.

HCHP is interested in fostering alternatives to traditional hospitalization. This is not necessarily cost-saving. The interest in alternatives derives from a desire to decrease dependence on traditional hospitals since, as pointed out above, hospital arrangements can be very complicated for an HMO such as HCHP. More important, however, is the belief that a day at home is better than a day in the hospital. Hospitals, after all, remain institutions despite efforts to personalize care within them. The challenges are to provide similar or better care outside the hospital and to market this care to the general population, who will be inclined to be skeptical about even shorter stays in the hospital.

An example of HCHP's interest in this area was its pilot programs to discharge newly delivered mothers within twenty-four hours of delivery which began in two centers in early 1985. In one, mothers were subsequently visited at home by a nurse practitioner who examined the baby and assessed the medical needs of mother and child. In the other, trained helpers came to the home for four days after discharge and performed several functions: they made sure that meals were available, did light housekeeping, and helped (as well as instructed when necessary) the mother with routine care of the newborn. This latter program has attracted more candidates than the former, although both have been satisfactorily received by those who have tried them. HCHP is now developing a plan-wide program which will combine the features of the two pilots.

It also is likely that HMOs and other institutions with an interest in decreasing their use of traditional hospitals will stimulate the acceptance, and perhaps even foster the development, of new technologies. The work of Dr. Gerald Moss,[4] who has discharged over 200 patients from the hospital within twenty-four hours of a cholecystectomy is being copied. Dr. Moss has developed some changes in technique which permit him to eliminate use of narcotic analgesics and to feed patients orally by the second day without development of ileus. Although it may take time to market the concept to physicians and patients, it is hard to believe that a patient who is home on the second day and visits Dr. Moss in his office on the third, is not doing better than the traditional cholecystectomy patient who is lucky to be discharged on the fifth or sixth day.

Physician Turnover

In HCHP's early years, physician turnover rates were low. For example, between 1978 and 1980, turnover in the plan's departments of internal medicine was 2–3 percent per year. In 1985, turnover in internal medicine was 5 percent. It is likely that the rates will be higher in the foreseeable future than they were in the past for several reasons: In the early years of HMO growth, including the 1970s, many physicians who accepted full-time positions in these organizations were intellectually committed to the concept of HMOs and prepaid care. They were unlikely to think of their positions as merely jobs. We have already mentioned that at HCHP the opportunity to examine candidates closely was greater when the plan was smaller. Similar opportunities are likely to occur in other small HMOs, even when they are not affiliated with teaching programs. As the quality of employment screening declines, it is likely that there will be a greater percentage of recruits who discover that they do not like to practice in the HMO setting and a greater percentage who do not live up to the HMO's standards and are asked to leave. Also, in the past physicians were less likely to be married to other professionals than they are now. When there is extensive hiring of young physicians, it is likely that there will be some turnover due to relocation of spouses as they complete training in their own professions, including medical training, or get caught up in the job mobility of early nonmedical careers.

The combination of higher physician turnover rates and leaves of absence, such as maternity leaves which are increasing as more women physicians join HMOs, makes it progressively more difficult to provide continuity of care to HMO members. Unfortunately, it appears likely that members of HMOs, such as HCHP, which have had a strong commitment to linking members with a primary care team, are going to have to accept some discontinuities in primary care clinicians; and HMOs are going to have to devise methods for making sure that the quality of care of these members remains high despite the discontinuities.

New Career Paths for Physicians in HMOs

As medicine becomes more "industrial" and as physicians increasingly become more likely to work in managed settings, the demand for physician-managers is likely to rise. HCHP has had a long commitment to an important managerial role for physicians. Each health center has a physician as health center director; and chiefs (who now number thirty-eight) are the general managers of their departments. The processes which need to be managed within departments are considerably less standardized than similar processes which occur in the traditional model of management in medicine—the teaching hospital department. Recruiting physicians who ideally will spend an entire career in one practice, evaluating what happens behind the closed office door, and developing new strengths in old staffs are challenging and complex tasks. At the same time, the chief must be an accomplished clinician and teacher. He or she must be able to motivate different types of clinicians to work well together and to work effectively with their support staffs; and the chief must be able to design and implement new programs to improve resource utilization, patient flow, etc. Perhaps because of the complexity and lack of standardization of the job which needs to be performed, the autocratic model so common in teaching hospitals is not particularly effective at HCHP. It has required considerable effort to train physicians to manage effectively, and several formal management programs have emerged.

Teaching is also likely to become an important function for physicians in ambulatory care settings such as HMOs.[5] As HMOs grow, it has become evident that the hospital plays only a small part in the total medical care of the patient and it also appears likely that the patient population for traditional teaching hospital-based education will be eroded. There does seem to be a growing interest in educating medical students and young postgraduate physicians in the elements of overall care of the patient; but there is not yet a clear scheme for merging the traditional interests of medical schools and teaching hospitals with the needs of HMOs and other practice settings to have well-trained practitioners. HCHP does have teaching as one of its goals. Teaching is conducted primarily through the auspices of the HCHP Teaching Program which is funded by the HCHP Foundation. The foundation is funded from a percentage of HCHP's revenues and uses these funds to support teaching, research, and community service. The director of the teaching program is a former medical director of HCHP. There is a teaching unit which is physically located within the Kenmore Center. It includes conference rooms, audiovisual facilities, rooms equipped with one-way mirrors or video-cameras for interviewing and examining real and simulated patients, a micro-computing facility, and a library. Several programs for medical students, house officers in affiliated teaching hospitals, fellows, and nurse practitioners are now run by the Teaching Program. There has also been a formal effort to improve and focus the teaching skills of HCHP clinicians. While it is likely that the HCHP Teaching Program will continue to grow and develop, it is not so likely that other HMOs, particularly the for-profit HMOs, will fund teaching activities from member premiums. If teaching within the HMO setting is to develop on a national scale, a number of problems need to be addressed to clarify the relationship of teaching to other activities at an HMO and the relationship of teaching within the HMO setting to the overall education of medical students and young physicians. These include: Who will be the teachers? What will be the incentives to teach? How will teachers be compensated? How will the HMO fund teaching activities? Will the funds come from external sources or from an appropriate quid pro quo to make it worthwhile to the HMO to sponsor teaching activities? What criteria will apply to the students to indicate that they have been educated appropriately (i.e., what will be the analog to current residency requirements)?

Overall, as long as the financing does not place it at a competitive disadvantage, teaching should have a beneficial effect on an HMO: clinician-teachers will have a stimulus to maintain high quality in their personal practices. The questioning attitude in a teaching setting should invigorate even those who do not participate directly in teaching. Not least, the students ultimately will be a more suitably trained source of new staff than currently exists. For these reasons, despite the unanswered questions above, it is probable that interest in improving educational opportunities within HMOs will continue to develop.

Standardization of Physician Practices

Another byproduct of the industrialization of medical practice is that demands are being placed on the new medical organizations that were rarely, if ever, placed on individual practitioners. One of these is that the parties who are paying for care, such as government agencies and employers, are increasingly interested in the quality of care provided. Although measurement of the quality of care remains a soft art, inroads are being made in assessing some of the components. Similarly, it is likely that in the future physicians will be expected to perform certain tasks according to standard. For example, there could easily be standards for immunization levels, for follow-up of abnormal screening test results such as Pap smears, and standards which define the components of a "checkup."

HCHP clearly seems headed in the direction of more standardization and measurement. There are relatively recently appointed physician-managers who are deputy medical director for health practices, with responsibility for development of practice standards, and vice-president for quality of care measurement (who reports directly to the president of HCHP). HCHP has long had an automated medical records system.[6]

This now includes a clinical reminder system. Components of this system do a variety of tasks aimed at standardization. For example, there is a reminder which is generated and sent to the clinician who obtained an abnormal Pap smear when there is no record of a follow-up examination within sixty days. Another type of reminder generates a listing of insulin-dependent diabetics every six months which indicates when they last had examinations such as ophthalmologic evaluations. A third type generates postcard reminders for patients whose age or diagnostic codes indicate that they are candidates for influenza vaccine. In addition, every time one of these persons has an appointment during the influenza vaccination season, a reminder is printed on the front of the printout of the record which is sent to the clinician. The same system makes it possible to evaluate each primary care practice at the end of the influenza season to determine the rates of influenza vaccination among suitable candidates.

Extrapolations from the Case Study

This chapter has provided a description of many of the features of physician staffing at HCHP. It is important to remember that HCHP is a staff model HMO, i.e., it is an example of the most tightly organized model of managed care settings. Relatively few staff model HMOs are being established at this time. They are capital intensive compared to IPAs; they are not suitable to the very high growth rates that have been sought and achieved in IPAs and PPOs; and they can be established only in populous areas. It remains to be seen what will become of staff model HMOs: They could occupy a valuable niche in the future world of health care; their anatomy could be unfavorable for the future world and become extinct; or they could develop different features from the ones they have today. In the meantime HMOs provide an interesting example of what can and cannot be achieved in managed care settings.

I believe that tightly organized care settings such as staff model HMOs generally and HCHP specifically have an opportunity to achieve a better standard of quality of care than less tightly organized care systems. In particular, if one compares a staff model HMO with fee-for-service practice, variation in care is less likely. While HMOs may not achieve the high peaks in quality of care found in some exceptional fee-for-service practices, it is also not likely to tolerate the deep valleys of quality that co-exist in the fee-for-service world. In the HMO it should be easier to identify and manage quality problems. Nevertheless, practice variations do exist, even within staff model HMOs and even when there are no economic incentives for such variations. For example, influenza vaccination rates at HCHP, measured by the reminder system described previously, have varied about threefold between practitioners with the poorest and best performance. This occurs despite the fact that the overall level of influenza immunization among high-risk members is higher than that reported in the general population.

Similarly, tightly organized HMOs are likely to be able to better manage the problems of impaired clinicians. Whereas, in the fee-for-service system it is often not clear who can or will blow the whistle or within whose jurisdiction the problem lies, be it alcoholism, drug-dependence, inappropriate sexual behavior, in an organized setting the problems are brought to the attention of the management. They cannot be swept under the rug; they must be managed.

A common public perception seems to be that physicians are just entrepreneurs. In contrast, physicians, as they are becoming involved in managed care settings, seem to perceive themselves increasingly as laborers. I believe that the public wants to perceive physicians neither as entrepreneurs nor laborers. Rather, the public is looking for physicians to be caring medical scientists. Just as the fee-for-service system is now failing, tightly organized settings will not succeed in the long run unless they provide what the public wants. The challenge for HMO managers is to foster the role of the caring physician and not to force or even allow physicians to feel like mere laborers. If we have well-motivated caring physicians, our members will be satisfied and the model will be perpetuated; if we do not, there will be call for further change.

HCHP has had to confront a number of important issues over the past sixteen years; and it is likely that most other managed care systems, even if they are not staff model HMOs will confront similar issues. These issues include staffing a rapidly growing organization with high quality clinicians; devising a mutually advantageous employment arrangement with appropriate incentives to achieve the desired kind of organization; utilizing nonphysician professionals in a way which is cost-effective and possibly expands the scope of services; training physicians to function in an environment which probably requires more use of new technology but less use of traditional hospital beds; providing continuity of care despite increasing physician turnover; developing physician-managers to run the industrialized medical world; and standardizing and monitoring medical care processes so that the public and their payers will be assured that they are the recipients of high quality care. Challenging though these tasks may be, none seems impossible; and the general population can only benefit as these tasks are addressed.

Notes

1. "What's in a Name?" *Harvard Medical Alumni Bulletin* 54 (1980): 14–28.

2. L. LeRoy, "The Cost and Effectiveness of Nurse Practitioners" (Washingon, D.C.: Office of Technology Assessment, Case Study No. 16, 1981).

3. Willard G. Manning et al., "A Controlled Trial of the Effect of a Prepaid Group Practice on Use of Services," *The New England Journal of Medicine* 310 (1984): 1505–1510.

4. Gerald Moss, Mary Ellen Regal, and Leo Lichtig, "Reducing Postoperative Pain, Narcotics, and Length of Hospitalization," *Surgery* 99 (1986): 206–209.

5. Gerald T. Perkoff, "Teaching Clinical Medicine in the Ambulatory Setting: An Idea Whose Time May Have Finally Come," *The New England Journal of Medicine* 314 (1986): 27–31.

6. Judith Golden, Margaret McCarthy, and Charles Suger, "User Comments: An Automated Medical Records System, Ten Years Later," *Proceedings of the Seventh Annual Symposium on Computer Applications in Medical Care* (New York: Institute of Electrical and Electronics Engineers, Computer Society Press, November 1983), pp. 77–79.

FIGURE 5.1
Harvard Community Health Plan Membership, 1969–1985

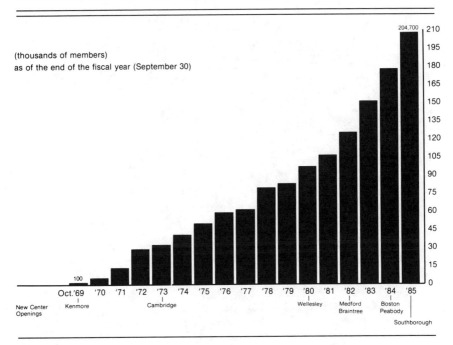

(thousands of members)
as of the end of the fiscal year (September 30)

(Courtesy of Harvard Community Health Plan)

FIGURE 5.2
Harvard Community Health Plan Enrollment Area

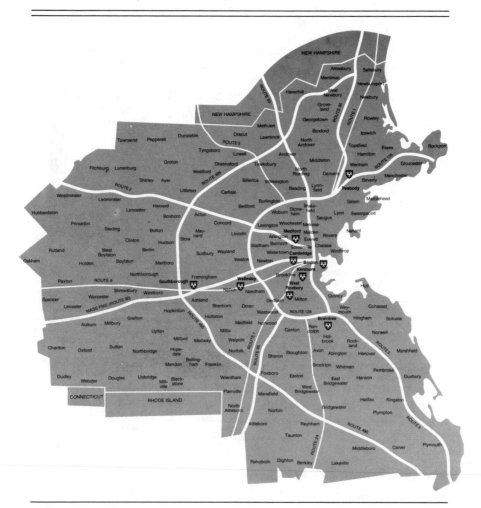

(Courtesy of Harvard Community Health Plan)

TABLE 5.1
Average Budgeted Physician Staffing Ratios*

	Ratio
Medical specialty	
Allergy	1:73,354
Dermatology	1:29,390
Adult neurology	1:60,245
Pediatric neurology	1:237,936
Gastroenterology	1:145,926
Endocrinology	1:184,071
Rheumatology	1:255,700
Pulmonary	1:452,078
Nephrology	1:516,071
Genetics	1:123,519
Surgical specialty	
Cardiology	1:113,020
Pediatric cardiology	1:452,078
Ophthalmology	1:25,892
Orthopedics	1:18,199
General surgery	1:21,928
ENT	1:32,690
Urology	1:59,275
Internal medicine	1:1,720**
Pediatrics	1:1,350***

Notes: *One full-time equivalent physician per "X" members.
    **Adult members (16 years of age or older).
  ***Child members.

6

A Lifestyle Decision: Facing the Reality of Physician Oversupply in the San Francisco Bay Area

Joan B. Trauner, Harold S. Luft, and Sandra S. Hunt

Introduction

To the visitor to San Franciso, "the city by the bay" is unique among America's cities because of its physical setting, climate, recreational and cultural facilities, and the diversity of its population. For physicians, San Francisco historically has been noted as a major medical teaching center—and as a highly desirable but extremely difficult city in which to establish a private practice. With 629.1 physicians per 100,000 population, San Francisco has the highest physician-to-population ratio in California and among the highest in the nation.[1] For the past ten to fifteen years, a decision to practice medicine in San Francisco has meant a conscious tradeoff of maximum income for lifestyle. The high cost of living in San Francisco translates into high operating expenses for a medical practice, while the decline in referrals from outlying communities, which today have a full complement of medical specialists, and the loss of patients to HMOs have created what is euphemistically referred to as "a patient shortage."

Until recently, the situation in the eight surrounding Bay Area counties has been quite the opposite. In contrast to the nominal population growth in San Francisco in the past twenty-five years, the outlying suburban areas have experienced explosive growth, and, thus, physicians entering these communities were able to establish practices with little difficulty. However, in the past few years, as the supply of physicians graduating from medical schools began to increase and as physicians trained in other areas of the country continued to settle in the Bay

Area, the physician-to-population figures for the other counties have jumped upward. According to 1983 data from the California Medical Association (CMA) (Table 6.1), Marin County, immediately north of San Francisco, now has the second highest physician-to-population ratio statewide, with 397.9 physicians per 100,000. Further north, Napa County, home of the wine industry, is number three with 301.1 physicians per 100,000, while Santa Clara (San Jose, Palo Alto), site of "Silicon Valley," is number five with 261.3 physicians. Across the Bay, Alameda County (Oakland) is number six with 248.1, and San Mateo County, immediately south of San Francisco, is number seven with 245.7. In other words, of all fifty-eight California counties, the San Francisco Bay Area has six out of the seven top slots; the only southern California county included in the top rankings is Los Angeles, in fourth position, with an overall physician-to-population ratio of 263.6.[2] As a group, the six largest counties in the San Francisco Bay area have a physician-to-population ratio of 308.0, compared to a statewide average of 235.5 and a national average of 188.2.[3]

Table 6.1 provides population estimates for the nine Bay Area counties, noting the number of active, nonfederal physicians practicing in each county, the number of physicians in office-based practice, and the percentage change in the physician supply by county for the periods of 1972–1982 and 1981–1983. As shown in the table, the percentage increase in physician population for the ten-year period between 1972–1982 was greatest in the counties of Solano (48.4 percent), Contra Costa (40.2 percent), San Mateo (37.5 percent), and Marin (36.7 percent). San Francisco had the third lowest growth rate (20.4 percent) for the ten-year period and the lowest growth rate (2.1 percent) for the period of 1981–1983.

Due to the physician influx throughout the Bay Area, today the awareness of a "patient shortage" is no longer restricted to San Francisco proper. With HMOs enrolling approximately 44 percent of the non-Medicare, non-Medicaid population in the nine Bay Area counties (Table 6.2), plus the increased physician supply, more and more physicians are recognizing that private practice, as it has existed in the past, is endangered. This chapter will examine the impact of the physician oversupply upon medical practice patterns in the San Francisco Bay Area. The focus will be on those changes that have occurred in the distribution of physicians and the organization and marketing of physician services. Much of the data for the analysis have been derived from studies conducted by the American Medical Association (AMA) and the California Medical Association (CMA), particularly as they relate to physician supply and specialty distribution. Data from the San Francisco Medical Society and Blue Shield of California were used to ascertain physician participation rates in Medicare, while information from three large multispecialty group practices, one staff model HMO, and the City and County of San Francisco, provided a perspective on salary levels in the Bay Area. Otherwise, financial data on medical practice were lacking since statistical data from such sources as the Internal Revenue Service and the AMA Physician Masterfile could not be disaggregated on the county or SMSA level. Thus, many of the findings reported in this chapter are based upon anecdotal information; at best, they provide an impressionistic analysis of practice trends in the San Francisco Bay Area.

The chapter begins with an overview of the general distribution of physicians in the San Francisco Bay Area. The next section describes some physician responses to competition, including participation in HMOs and preferred provider organizations (PPOs), use of advertising, and Medicare participation rates. A third section looks briefly at the emergence of new medical practice forms and the increasing competition between physician-sponsored and hospital-sponsored programs. A concluding section discusses the implications of new practice trends for the future of health care delivery in the Bay Area.

Physician Distribution
in the San Francisco Bay Area

Measuring the Existing Physician Supply

As shown in Tables 6.1 and 6.3, San Francisco not only has the highest overall physician-to-population ratio in the San Francisco Bay Area but the highest percentage of physicians in training, administration, and teaching/research positions. Only 61 percent of physicians in San Francisco are in office- or hospital-based practice, compared to a Bay Area average of 74.4 percent. Even when compared to other counties where medical schools are located (Table 6.4), this low percentage of office- and hospital-based physicians still remains; only one other county (the sparsely populated San Bernardino, home of Loma Linda University, at 62.3 percent) approaches the level of San Francisco. Thus, San Francisco acts as a "reservoir" of medical talent, providing for a steady infusion of young professionals into the greater Bay Area—and throughout Northern California.

When the physician-to-population ratio for office- and hospital-based physicians is calculated (Table 6.3), San Francisco still continues to have the highest concentration of physicians in practice within the Bay Area (383.9 physicians per 100,000, compared to a Bay Area average of 218.3). Analysis of the age distribution of physicians within the office-

and hospital-based category shows that the percentage of physicians under age thirty-five (17.2 percent) is highest in San Francisco of the nine Bay Area counties; a similar pattern emerges when San Francisco is compared to the six other counties in the state with medical schools (Table 6.4). Considering the overall low growth rate in the physician supply in San Francisco over the past ten years (Table 6.1) compared to other Bay Area counties, this finding is rather remarkable.

A statistical artifact may partly account for the concentration of young physicians in San Francisco proper. The AMA assigns physicians to a county of practice on the basis of their professional mailing address, which may be a residence or office location. Many physicians—particularly when they are in training and rotating through a series of hospitals—register using their residence, and this same situation may continue after they complete their training. Thus, there is the possibility that the concentration of young physicians in San Francisco reflects the continuing popularity of San Francisco as a place to live—rather than as a place to practice medicine. However, a reverse commute to outside the city is still relatively uncommon and is not likely to produce the numbers necessary to create the relatively large supply of physicians under the age of thirty-five.

To help explain the under age of thirty-five trend, data on the employment status of physicians (i.e., salaried, individual or partnership, professional corporation) and data on participation in medical groups at the county level would have been helpful; however, there was no readily available source for this information. There is the possibility that part of the influx of young physicians into practice within San Francisco is attributable to salaried employment or group practice. It is known that physicians accepting salaried positions with the Kaiser Permanente Medical Group and other hospital-based or staff model HMOs (e.g., French Hospital in San Francisco) are included in the private practice totals. There is some evidence to suggest that these types of salaried positions—particularly at Kaiser—have become the new "plums" for physicians completing their residency training. For example, of the physicians completing the general internal medicine residency at the University of California San Francisco (UCSF) in 1984 and 1985, each year two out of six joined Kaiser-San Francisco and others joined Kaiser groups in other Bay Area locations. While complete information on the practice whereabouts of the 1984 internal medicine residents is unavailable, it is known that none of the 1985 class entered private practice in the San Francisco Bay Area. Other types of salaried employment available in San Francisco include positions at hospital-sponsored HMOs, freestanding urgent care centers, and industrial clinics.

Not only do AMA data show that San Francisco has the highest percentage of physicians under age thirty-five, but conversely, it has the highest concentration of physicians aged sixty-five and over in practice within the Bay Area (Table 6.3). Again, considering the high costs of practice in San Francisco—particularly salary, rent scales, and malpractice costs—one would expect that older physicians, in face of declining patient loads, would opt for early retirement. There are several possible explanations for the large number of physicians who continue to practice past the age of sixty-four. The first is that given the high cost of living in San Francisco, many physicians cannot afford to retire. Some physicians may not have adequate funds for retirement, while others—in locations with low overhead and/or in specialties with low malpractice costs—may choose to continue to practice as a hedge against future inflation. Some physicians may continue to practice and carry a full patient load, while others may reduce their hours or limit their practices to consulting. Finally, others may obtain salaried positions as medical directors with large national or state firms headquartered in San Francisco or with insurance carriers and with peer/utilization review organizations. To the extent that salaried physicians are not assigned to an "administrative" classification in the AMA records, then the percentage of physicians sixty-five and over in private practice may be somewhat overinflated.

The age distribution statistics for the other Bay Area counties reveal some unusual patterns. Table 6.3 shows that Marin and Napa counties, which rank second and third statewide in terms of their physician-to-population ratios, are relatively inhospitable sites for starting a medical practice. Marin has 8.5 percent and Napa, 5.8 percent of their office- and hospital-based physicians in the thirty-five-and-under category. Marin has one major multispecialty group practice other than Kaiser, and applications for positions with this group have been so great that quoted salary rates for most entry-level physicians have either been held constant or lowered slightly over the past few years. In Napa, there are no multispecialty practices other than Kaiser. Neither Napa nor Marin has extensive industrial or commercial development, and thus there is no source of salaried income to supplement earnings from private practice during the start-up years.

When standards developed in 1980 by the Graduate Medical Education National Advisory Committee (GMENAC) are used to evaluate physician supply, Marin is 213.1 percent and Napa is 161.3 percent above recommended levels (Table 6.5). For primary care, defined as family/general practitioners, internists, obstetricians/gynecologists, and pediatricians, the ratios in Marin and Napa drop to 130.5 percent and 107.6 percent, respectively; thus, the bulk of the oversupply results from an overconcentration of specialists. Young physicians trained as specialists who wish to begin practice in these counties not only have to establish referral patterns among older colleagues, but they probably have to contend with "turf invasion"—the delivery of services by physicians outside their designated specialties. As a result, Marin and Napa counties are relatively forbidding places to begin a private practice.[4] They are, however, highly desirable areas in which to live, with Marin having the highest median family income in the Bay Area and reportedly the highest concentration of physician residences (Table 6.6).

As for the other communities, only one of the counties, Solano, falls below recommended GMENAC standards in its total physician supply. In this case, Solano County has not experienced the extensive industrial development characteristic of the San Francisco Bay Area; it has only one major city, Vallejo, with a population of 89,000 and no tertiary hospitals. Moreover, Solano has the lowest per capita income of the nine Bay Area counties according to the 1980 census (Table 6.6). For Solano, there is a deficit across both the primary care and surgical specialty categories (Table 6.5). There are three other counties that show a deficit in the supply of primary care physicians, ranging from considerable (Contra Costa, 74.4 percent of recommended standards) to slight (Santa Clara, 98.8 percent). When the recommended GMENAC standards are calculated for nine surgical specialties, Contra Costa is the only county, other than Solano, to show a deficit. Conversely, three counties show large oversupplies of primary care physicians (Alameda, Marin, and San Francisco) and seven have an excess of surgical specialists.

Entering Practice

Physicians who wish to enter practice in the Bay Area generally hear about positions through contact with faculties and teaching staffs in medical schools, residency programs and/or local hospitals, and direct application to group practices and HMOs. An analysis of advertisements in the CMA's *Physician Placement Bulletin* in the November/December issues of 1977, 1983, and 1985 (Table 6.7) revealed virtually no advertising from two of the six largest Bay Area counties (Marin and San Mateo) over the eight-year period and declines in the four others (San Francisco, Alameda, Contra Costa, and Santa Clara). By 1985, only in Santa Clara County was there any meaningful choice of advertised positions. In contrast, the number of advertisements remained at a relatively high level for the rural counties of the state throughout the period.

When the sources of the CMA advertisements were tallied, other trends became apparent. Whereas staff/group model HMOs were regularly advertising for physicians in 1977, HMO advertisements had disappeared by 1983 and 1985. There is anecdotal evidence to suggest that in earlier years, some HMOs had difficulties in recruiting board-eligible internists and surgical specialists, particularly those trained at prestigious universities. However, as the HMO market share grew and the supply of physicians increased, this situation changed markedly. The assumption can be made that because of the increased supply of physicians and a changing attitude towards salaried employment, the HMOs had a sufficient applicant pool by the early 1980s to eliminate the need for further advertising. During the same period, considerable declines were also noted for ads placed by solo or two-person practices, small groups (three to nine physicians, single or multispecialty), and hospitals. Only group practices (single or multispecialty) with ten or more physicians recorded an increase. Overall, the number of advertisements for positions in the Bay Area dropped from a high of fifty in 1977 to thirty-one in 1983 and twenty-one in 1985.

The lack of private practice opportunities, in turn, has helped to mold career decisions of medical students and residents in training in the San Francisco Bay Area. For example, in 1980 when private practice opportunities were still available in some communities, 54.2 percent of UCSF medical school graduates intended to enter private practice compared to a nationwide average of 65.4 percent.[5] This lower response rate was primarily due to the larger number of UCSF students reporting interest in full-time academic practice (28.1 percent compared to 20.2 percent nationwide); only a slightly higher percentage of UCSF graduates in 1980 favored salaried clinic practice compared to the U.S. average (13.6 percent compared to 11.7 percent nationwide). By 1985, however, the percentage of UCSF students intending to enter private practice had dropped precipitously to 32.0 percent, while the national average was 57.9 percent.[6] The percentage of UCSF graduates expressing interest in salaried practice had jumped to 24.6 percent and for full-time academic practice had climbed to 38.3 percent compared to national averages of 12.0 percent and 27.6 percent, respectively.

Physician Responses to Increased Competition

As previously noted, physicians in the Bay Area—and San Francisco in particular—have long been aware of increased competition for patients. According to a study conducted by the CMA in the winter of 1981-1982, 69.9 percent of the 1,370 respondents practicing in the major metropolitan areas of the state perceived that there was a physician oversupply. Of all the counties in the state, the highest rate of positive responses about the presence of an oversupply were recorded for Marin (94.1 percent of respondents) and San Francisco (90.2 percent). The CMA published findings did not include a geographic breakdown of responses by medical specialty, but statewide, the perception of an oversupply was highest among surgical specialists, with 85.7 percent of plastic surgeons reporting an oversupply, followed by ophthalmologists (79.3 percent), urologists (75.8 percent), and otolaryngologists (70.7 percent). The specialty least likely to see an oversupply was general/family practitioners (33.5 percent), whereas a majority of other primary care providers—internists (60.8 percent), obstetricians/gynecologists (59.5 percent), and pediatricians (60.2 percent)—reported an oversupply.[7]

The CMA survey also looked at how physicians were responding to the increase in the number of practicing physicians. Of the 1,370 physicians practicing in major metropolitan areas, 44.1 percent reported use of advertising/public relations for some aspect of their practice; 59.6 percent reported providing services outside their specialty; 61.3 percent reported accepting referrals from more sources; 52.9 percent reported accepting categories of patients not previously treated (e.g., workers' compensation, legal consultation, Medi-Cal); and 66.5 percent reported a greater willingness to enter into agreements (e.g., with HMOs) with payments below "usual and customary" levels of reimbursement. However, only 8.2 percent reported lowering their regular fees in response to the changing market for physician services.[8]

Despite increasing competition, there is some evidence that although physicians may have attended marketing seminars and may have re-tailored their practices to attract more patients (e.g., by extending office hours, processing insurance claims), most remained relatively conservative in their use of advertising in most parts of the Bay Area. For example, in *The Silver Pages*, a directory issued by Southwestern Bell Media, Inc. for senior citizens in San Francisco, only seventy-three physicians, out of a total of approximately 2,500 active physicians, took out advertisements. Of this number, fifteen advertised taking assignment without mention of discounts or free initial consultations; fourteen announced acceptance of assignment as payment in full; seven physicians offered a free initial office visit or screening, without mention of assignment or discount; thirty-six physicians offered some form of discount, either as a percentage off of fees or as a specific dollar amount off of office visits; and one physician offered free medicines.

Similarly, within the San Francisco *Yellow Pages* of the *Pacific Bell Telephone Directory* (1985-1986), there were only twelve display ads for individual physician practices, of which five were for plastic surgeons. The bulk of the large-scale advertisements were for freestanding facilities, including a series of announcements for drop-in office practices, urgent care centers, and sports medicine/executive physical centers in the financial district. One new development in the *Yellow Pages* was the appearance of physician referral networks. Historically, the San Francisco

Medical Society operated the major referral program in the city. The 1985-1986 *Directory* listed sixteen referral services, of which seven were hospital-sponsored, one represented a referral service in the gay community, and the remainder were for specialty-type services (e.g., plastic surgery, vision care, house calls, and allergy).

There is evidence that instead of paying for advertisements to attract patients, a growing number of Bay Area physicians are marketing their services through participation in multiple preferred provider and HMO arrangements. In September–October 1983, the CMA conducted a sample survey of its members to ascertain their participation rate in IPAs and PPOs. Of 564 respondents in large metropolitan areas, 160 or 28.4 percent belonged to an IPA; of this number, 65 or 40.6 percent received more than 5 percent of their patients from an IPA. In San Francisco, Marin, Santa Clara, and San Mateo, the reported IPA participation rates were 46.8, 45.5, 47.8, and 55.6 percent respectively, nearly twice the statewide metropolitan rate.[9]

The survey looked at PPO contracting, but because contracting was still in its early stages and because of the low number of respondents who had actually signed agreements (26 percent out of a total of 762 respondents statewide), no breakdown was provided by geographic area of the state. However, in 1985 the California Hospital Association (CHA) identified ninety-five PPOs operating in California, of which sixty responded to a CHA survey. Six insurance companies reported signing a total of 82,072 physician contracts; the forty-nine other PPOs that supplied information reported a total of 57,496 physician contracts. The CHA survey reported ten PPOs operating in Santa Clara, seven in San Francisco, Marin, San Mateo, Alameda, and Contra Costa counties, and four in Napa, Sonoma, and Solano counties.[10] The study did not provide an unduplicated physician count by geographic area.[11] (Another thirty-five PPOs identified by the CHA did not respond to the survey.)

Some of the PPOs have solicited physicians through blanket mailings within a defined service area; others have created hospital networks and then limited participation to the medical staff at participating hospitals. Today, some of the large, full-service hospitals in the Bay Area report having as many as twenty-five to forty PPO contracts, with a few reporting as many as seventy. (PPOs organized by hospital chains/ networks, brokers, consultants, and third-party administrators often have conducted separate negotiations and developed different contract terms and/or provider networks for each of their large clients.) Preliminary evidence indicates that there is considerable overlap in physician panels for many of the PPOs. For example, an examination of the crossover between physicians participating in the Pru-Net program (Prudential) and the Prudent Buyer program (Blue Cross) in San Francisco found that of 284 physicians listed in the Pru-Net directory, 154 were also included in the Prudent Buyer program. The crossover rate was almost 100 percent in the medical and surgical subspecialties, with lower rates for physicians involved in primary care.

The age distribution for Prudent Buyer physician members in San Francisco, Santa Clara, and Marin counties by date of graduation from medical school is shown in Table 6.8. When the distribution is compared with the age breakdowns in Table 6.5, physicians in the youngest two categories are significantly more likely to participate in the Blue Cross program, while those in the older age groups are significantly less likely to participate, again confirming that younger physicians must take added measures to increase their patient bases.[12] When physicians participating in both the Prudent Buyer program and the Pru-Net program in San Francisco are compared with those participating only in the Prudent Buyer program, there are no significant differences in the age breakdowns. This finding suggests that once physicians decide to join a single PPO, they are willing to join other PPOs as well, regardless of their age.

Finally, another way of evaluating physician attitudes is to determine their assignment rates and their willingness to sign up for the Medicare Part B Participation Program. Physician assignment rates reportedly have been linked to the following: patient income (the higher the income, the less willing the physician is to accept assignment); physician specialty (the higher the charge per procedure, the more willing a physician is to accept assignment); local competition, especially from HMOs marketing coverage to Medicare eligibles; and the presence of strong consumer groups that publish physician directories. Table 6.9 provides information on physician participation rates by specialty in San Francisco County. Overall, the participation rate for the period of October 1984–September 1985 was 44.1 percent, compared to a national average of 29.8 percent.[13] For the surgical specialties, the participation rate was 49.4 percent; for general/family practice, 48.9 percent; and for medical specialties, 32.9 percent, compared to a national average of 32.4, 27.6, and 29.2 percent, respectively.[14] In other words, San Francisco physicians were more likely to accept assignment on all claims than their colleagues elsewhere, suggesting that they fear losing patients to competitors. When participation rates for specific specialties are examined, the figures ranged from a low of no participation for proctologists, 3.9 percent for anesthesiologists, and 5.7 percent for radiologists, to a high of 91.7 percent for pulmonary disease specialists, 79.4 percent for psychiatrists, 78.9 percent for neurosurgeons, and 72.7 percent for cardiovascular surgeons.

Table 6.10 provides the distribution of assignment rates for nonparticipating physicians in 1983 and for individual (non-group) physicians submitting 100 or more claims in 1982 (prior to the advent of the Part

B Participation Program). In 1982, 42.8 percent of 1,210 San Francisco physicians submitting 100 or more Medicare claims accepted assignment 50 percent of the time. Data for 1983 show an increase in overall use of assignment with 63.7 percent either participating in the Medicare program or accepting assignment 50 percent or more of the time. When data for members of the San Francisco Medical Society (SFMS) are examined, these physicians had a lower rate of participation ($p = <0.05$) as well as fewer physicians accepting assignment for 90–100 percent of claims in 1983. There was no significant difference in the age distribution of SFMS members for ages thirty-five to sixty-five and the totals for active office- and hospital-based physicians in San Francisco, but the numbers were lower in the under thirty-five and higher in the over sixty-five categories. Because information is unavailable on practice status (solo, partnership, group, professional corporation, salaried) of SFMS members, as well as the total physician population, it was impossible to determine if practice status was a major determinant of the difference in participation/assignment rates. Similarly, the age of physicians participating in Medicare has not been determined for either SFMS members or the total active, office- and hospital-based physician population in San Francisco.

Table 6.11 provides data on Medicare assignment/participation rates for internists, ophthalmologists, and clinics/group practices in four of the large Bay Area counties. In Marin and Santa Clara, the two high-income counties as measured by median family income (Table 6.6), the assignment rate for individual physicians and groups/clinics was considerably below that in San Francisco and Alameda.

Emergence of New Delivery Systems

The preceding sections have focused primarily upon physician responses to the increased competition resulting from an oversupply of health professionals in the Bay Area. One outcome of this competition has been that young physicians entering practice have been willing to accept a guaranteed income, by signing up for salaried positions, as a tradeoff for the potential long-term benefits of developing their own practices. An AMA survey, for example, found that in 1983, 39 percent of practicing physicians in the under age thirty-six category[15] were salaried, compared to 23 percent between ages thirty-six and forty-five.[16] This trend, in turn, created a highly favorable hiring situation for large multispecialty group practices and HMOs.

Table 6.12 provides income data for one large multispecialty group practice, across specialties, and limited data for three others, plus the city and county of San Francisco. Readily evident is the fact that most groups in the San Francisco Bay Area offer rates below national averages. For example, with the exception of one full professor leaving a medical school faculty, the starting salaries for internists at the three listed groups were in the range of $50,000–$60,000 in 1985. Even the city and county of San Francisco, historically known for its low salary structure, offered comparable rates. In comparison, the latest available data from the AMA, using 1983 information, showed the average income for a practicing internist on the Pacific Coast was $90,100 and for a young physician under age thirty-six, the national average was $68,000. Comparison of salaries for one large Bay Area multispecialty group (Group A) with the under age thirty-six category for the other specialties for which AMA data were available, showed that their rates were comparable with national averages for obstetrics/gynecology and psychiatry, higher for pediatrics, and considerably lower for anesthesiology and general surgery. In other words, Group A has begun to realign practice income across specialties. For example, physicians trained in general surgery, a highly overcrowded specialty in the Bay Area, no longer command a premium salary. At Group A, general surgeons are on the same pay scale as primary care providers (internists and pediatricians) and psychiatrists. Obstetricians/gynecologists, otolaryngologists, and emergency room physicians are hired at the next salary level ($72,000–$76,200), while premium salaries are reserved for the two fields—anesthesiology and orthopedics—where recruitment of physicians to group practices and HMOs remains relatively difficult. In evaluating Group A salaries, it is important to note that the income for all practitioners, except emergency room physicians, was held constant for the last two years, and there were limited salary increases in 1984 for all fields, except anesthesiology and orthopedics.

In the Bay Area, the success of large multispecialty group practices in securing contracts with HMOs, such as Take Care (Blue Cross) and Maxicare, and the general interest on the part of hospitals in developing joint ventures with their medical staffs for risk contracts under Medicare and various preferred provider/exclusive provider arrangements, has spawned new interest in closed panel, independent practice associations (IPAs). For example, in one Bay Area hospital which has a preferred provider relationship with a large electronics firm, the Preferred Physicians Medical Group, Inc. is evolving into an IPA. The hospital is currently developing a prepaid health plan and preparing an application for a Medicare risk contract. Eventually, the physician group will deliver services under a capitated arrangement with the newly formed HMO. Included in the IPA are medical staff physicians who belong to a large multispecialty group practice in the same area—a group practice which itself has a capitated arrangement with Take Care and Maxicare.[17] At the same time, physicians participating in the Preferred Physicians Medical Group (including those in the multispecialty group practice) remain members of a county-wide IPA, originally organized as an offshoot of the local Foundation for Medical Care. Thus, multiple allegiances to a series of alternative delivery systems is one of the emerging characteristics of medical practice in the Bay Area.

A new phenomenon which has appeared in San Francisco, where to date there have been no large multispecialty fee-for-service group practices, is the quasi-medical group. Designed to compete against hospital-sponsored urgent care centers, sports facilities, and industrial clinics, a quasi-medical group involves the sharing of office space in a single location (often a nonmedical office building in the financial district). These quasi-groups differ from physician practices in traditional medical office buildings in that the physicians have created a closed panel referral system, in which participants are required to maintain specific office hours and offer a defined set of services. Usually, these groups do not share income or operating expenses, but they do provide for joint advertising and marketing programs.

Future Trends

The Bay Area, as elsewhere in the nation, has seen growing competition between hospital-sponsored programs (e.g., women's health centers, health fairs, worksite screening programs, drop-in clinics/urgent care centers, weight control programs, sports centers, etc.) and traditional office practice. In addition, the continued growth of HMOs and PPOs, and the appearance of Medicare risk contracting have fostered a growing sense of panic among many Bay Area physicians. Those physicians who have refused to participate in alternative delivery systems are slowly backing off from this stand. For example, the Prudent Buyer program (Blue Cross), which initially had difficulties in recruiting physicians in a number of specialties, has seen its statewide enrollment increase by 270 percent since its inception in 1983. Without any encouragement from Blue Cross, physicians have voluntarily submitted contracts, requesting to be listed in the *Prudent Buyer Directory* as preferred providers. Similarly, Blue Shield of California has seen an increase in the number of its physician members since the advent of its PPO, with the total rising from approximately 24,000 in 1980 to 36,000 in 1986.[18]

Despite the fears of most physicians regarding loss of patients to alternative delivery systems, there has been only limited support in the Bay Area for the physician-union concept. In 1983, shortly after passage of PPO-enabling legislation, the Union of American Physicians and Dentists (UAPD), which is headquartered in Oakland, attempted to capitalize on anti-PPO sentiment to recruit additional members. In April 1983, the UAPD filed suit against Blue Cross, arguing that its PPO was an "illegal exercise of its dominant, controlling position in the insurance market" and that creation of the PPO constituted "an illegal monopoly act."[19] Despite repeated mailings detailing acts by various insurance carriers, by HMOs, by government—and even by organized medicine—to undermine physician autonomy, union membership has remained relatively limited. As of January 1985, the UAPD estimated that its total physician membership in California was 12,000, of which an estimated 35–40 percent were salaried physicians (often in state government positions).

What does the future hold for medical practice in the San Francisco Bay Area? Six important trends can be discerned. First, physicians will continue to sign up with HMOs and PPOs on a willy-nilly basis in the hopes of preserving their patient bases. However, in the long run, participation in a series of alternative delivery systems—with different billing rates and requirements for utilization review—will tax their administrative capabilities. Therefore, they will either look more favorably upon various forms of group practice as a way of improving their efficiency or, if they remain in solo/partnership practice, they will do most of their contracting through an IPA—possibly one that is hospital-based. Second, as the hospitals that are the "winners" and "losers" for PPO and HMO contracts become apparent, physicians at these facilities will tighten up requirements for medical staff privileges to preserve their market dominance. Third, the tightening up of staff privileges will make entry into medical practice in the Bay Area increasingly more difficult for young physicians. Fourth, as gatekeeper systems using primary care providers proliferate, there will be reduced demand for many specialty services. Fifth, the existing oversupply of specialists and the reduced demand for their services will permit a further narrowing of the income differential between primary care physicians and specialists, particularly for young physicians joining medical groups. Sixth, the pending mergers among a number of Bay Area hospitals will ultimately lead to closure of specialized units and regionalization of new high-cost technologies; this trend will, in turn, reduce the practice opportunities for young physicians. In other words, practice in the Bay Area will remain a tradeoff between income and lifestyle, with more limited practice choices—in terms of location and conditions of employment—for the entering physician.

Notes

1. California Medical Association, "Physician Supply in California, 1983," *CMA Socioeconomic Report* (forthcoming, Spring 1986).

2. Whereas the boundaries of San Francisco City and County are coterminous, Los Angeles County, because of its vast size, is composed of many communities with wide variations in physician-to-population ratios. Presumably, the averages for communities such as West Los Angeles and Beverly Hills are considerably higher than the county-wide average, and may approach the levels of the top-ranking counties in the Bay Area.

3. Population figures for the San Francisco Bay Area may include data from five, six, or nine counties, depending upon whether Santa Clara in the South Bay, and Sonoma, Napa, and Solano in the North Bay, are included in the totals. Except for Table 6.1 where population ratios for six counties and nine counties are noted, the remainder of the tables in this report provide summary data only for the nine counties. National and state data are from American Medical Association, *Physician Characteristics and Distribution in the United States*, 1983 edition (Chicago: AMA, 1983).

4. California, Department of Finance, *State Census Data Center Newsletter* 3 (1983): 3. Median family income is based upon 1980 census data as revised by the State Census Data Center.

5. Association of American Medical Colleges, Graduation Questionnaire, 1980.

6. Association of American Medical Colleges, Graduation Questionnaire, 1985.

7. Roger J. Purdy, "Physician Supply—An Assessment by California Medical Association Members (Part 1)," *CMA Socioeconomic Report* 23 (1983): 1–8.

8. Roger J. Purdy, "Physician Supply—An Assessment by California Medical Association Members (Part 2)," *CMA Socioeconomic Report* 24 (1984): 1–10.

9. The number of respondents in all four Bay Area counties was fewer than fifty physicians. See Michael W. Jones, "Physician Contracting Activities, 1983," *CMA Socioeconomic Report* 24 (1984): 1–8.

10. The number of PPOs relates to contracting entities, rather than the number of actual contracts offered by each program.

11. Cindy Arstein-Kerslake, "PPOs—The New Delivery System," *CHA Insight* 9 (1985): 1–4.

12. The funding of physician participation in PPOs being age-related has been confirmed on a national level. See M. Roy Schwarz, "Physician Personnel and Physician Practice," in Eli Ginzberg, ed., *From Physician Shortage to Patient Shortage: The Uncertain Future of Medical Practice* (Boulder, Co.: Westview Press, 1986).

13. Ira Burney and George Schieber, "Medicare Physicians' Services: The Composition of Spending and Assignment Rates," *Health Care Financing Review* 7(1985): 81–96.

14. Jerry Cromwell and Margot Rosenbach, *An Analysis of Medicare's Physician Participating Agreement Program; Report Submitted to Health Care Financing Administration for National Opinion Research Center Contract*, Appendix B, Table B-3 (forthcoming, 1986).

15. Roger A. Reynolds and Daniel T. Dunn, eds., *1984 Socioeconomic Characteristics of Medical Practice* (Chicago: AMA, 1984). The AMA uses two different age breakdowns in its publications. In *Physician Characteristics and Distribution in the United States*, physician age is divided at thirty-four and

under, and in *Socioeconomic Characteristics of Medical Practice*, the split is made at thirty-five and under.

16. David Wessel, "Rx for Medics: More Young Doctors Shun Private Practice, Work as Employees," *Wall Street Journal*, 13 January 1986, pp. 1, 17.

17. The multispecialty group, as an entity, does not participate in the hospital-associated PPO; rather, its member physicians have the option of participating, as individuals, in the program.

18. Personal communication with Ralph Schaffarzick, M.D., Senior Vice President and Medical Director, Blue Shield of California, February 25, 1986.

19. Union of American Physicians and Dentists v. Blue Cross of California, San Francisco Superior Court, Case #808449, 29 April 1983.

TABLE 6.1
Physician/Population Ratios, San Francisco Bay Area

County	Total Active MDs	Office-based Physicians[2] #	Office-based Physicians[2] %	1983 Population[3] (000)	Number 1983	County Rank, 1983	Percentage Change 1972–82	Percentage Change 1981–83
San Francisco	4,421	2,520	57.0	702.7	629.1	1	20.4	2.1
Marin	887	684	77.1	222.9	397.9	2	36.7	5.7
Napa	305	217	71.1	101.3	301.1	3	11.6	5.9
Santa Clara	3,547	2,512	70.8	1,357.5	261.3	5	18.1	5.0
Alameda	2,860	2,175	76.0	1,153.0	248.1	6	23.1	8.1
San Mateo	1,480	1,117	75.5	602.4	245.7	7	37.5	10.6
Contra Costa	1,396	1,132	81.1	691.7	201.8	13	40.2	6.1
Sonoma	633	513	81.0	322.3	196.4	16	30.0	7.7
Solano	305	220	72.1	251.4	121.3	39	48.4	2.7
BAY AREA								
Six counties[4]	14,591	10,140	69.5	4,732.2	308.0		29.4	5.4
Nine counties	15,834	11,090	70.0	5,412.2	292.6		29.5	5.4
CALIFORNIA	59,151	43,060	72.8	25,116.0	235.5			

Physicians per 100,000 population[1]

Notes:
[1] Physicians per 100,000 population include all active, nonfederal physicians including interns, residents, medical teaching, research, and administration.
[2] Office-based physicians include physicians in private and group practice, but excludes interns, residents, and physicians involved primarily in teaching, research, and administration.
[3] State population estimates differ from county population estimates. State total excludes non-civilians.
[4] Excluded from the total are the North Bay counties of Napa, Sonoma, and Solano.

Source: California Medical Association (CMA), Bureau of Research and Planning.

136

TABLE 6.2
HMO Market Penetration, San Francisco Bay Area

County	Estimated Pop. 1/85[1]	Medicare Pop. 7/85[2]	%	Adjusted MediCal Pop. 7/84[3]	%	Net Population Under 65 w/o MediCal
Alameda	1,174,800	127,389	10.8	106,927	9.1	940,484
Contra Costa	703,400	75,717	10.8	46,212	6.6	581,471
Marin	223,200	25,373	11.4	5,795	2.6	192,032
Napa	102,200	17,240	16.9	5,549	5.4	79,411
San Francisco	719,200	109,381	15.2	63,144	8.8	546,675
San Mateo	606,200	74,987	12.4	16,859	2.8	514,354
Solano	269,100	22,100	8.2	18,859	7.0	228,141
Santa Clara	1,376,900	189,545	13.8	83,050	6.0	1,104,305
Sonoma	333,000	45,862	13.8	21,687	6.5	265,451
Total	5,508,000	687,594		368,082		4,452,324

HMO Enrollment (non-Medicare/non-MediCal):[4] 1,949,718 (43.79%)

Notes:

[1]Population estimates (January 1985) from California Department of Finance, Population Research Unit.

[2]Medicare population estimates from Health Care Financing Administration Region IX.

[3]MediCal population, less Medicare eligibles, from California Department of Health Services, Medical Care Statistics Unit, *MediCal Eligible Report*, July 1984.

[4]HMO enrollment statistics, with exception of Kaiser, are from InterStudy, Excelsior, Minnesota (July 1985 data); Kaiser Foundation Health Plan statistics have been adjusted to remove enrollment in Sacramento region. Plans included in total are: Kaiser-North, Take Care, Bay Pacific, Lifeguard, Heals, HealthAmerica, Institute of Preventive Medicine, Health Plan of America, Children's French, Maxicare, and Contra Costa Health Plan.

TABLE 6.3
Active Physicians with Patient Care Responsibilities, by Age

County	N Active Physicians[1]	N Office Hospital-based[2]	% Office and Hospital-based Pop.	ratio	Office and Hospital-based				
					% <35	% 35-44	% 45-54	% 55-64	% 65+
Alameda	2,860	2,310	80.8	200.3	13.2	35.4	23.5	18.5	9.5
Contra Costa	1,396	1,202	86.1	173.8	12.2	37.6	25.3	18.1	6.8
Marin	887	718	80.9	322.1	8.5	38.0	28.3	18.9	6.3
Napa	305	275	81.0	271.5	5.8	33.5	23.6	26.9	10.2
San Francisco	4,421	2,698	61.0	383.9	17.2	30.4	23.0	17.6	11.8
San Mateo	1,480	1,168	78.9	193.9	13.7	27.6	26.1	22.8	9.8
Santa Clara	3,574	2,641	73.9	194.5	13.7	31.6	28.7	20.0	6.1
Solano	305	238	78.0	94.7	16.4	37.4	17.6	20.6	8.0
Sonoma	633	553	87.4	171.6	12.8	42.9	20.1	16.3	8.0
Bay Area range[3]	15,861	11,803	74.4	218.3					

Notes:
[1]Excluded from the totals are physicians classified as "inactive."
[2]Includes office and hopsital-based physicians, but excludes residents and physicians involved in teaching, administration, research, and "other" activities.
[3]Includes data for nine counties.

Source: American Medical Association (AMA), Division of Survey and Data Resources, Physician Masterfile for 1983, September 1985. Table 11.

TABLE 6.4
Active Physicians with Patient Care Responsibilities, by Age, in Counties with Medical Schools

County	# Active[1]	# Office & Hospital-based[2]	% Office & Hospital-based[3]	Office & Hospital-based Physicians				
				% <35	% 35-44	% 45-54	% 55-64	% 65+
San Francisco	4421	2698	61.0	17.2	30.4	23.0	17.6	11.8
Los Angeles	20670	15485	74.9	14.4	30.6	23.0	20.1	11.9
Orange	4753	3928	82.6	13.6	36.9	26.7	17.0	5.9
Sacramento	1967	1469	74.7	16.0	34.9	24.9	17.8	6.4
San Diego	4641	3564	76.8	13.7	38.4	23.4	17.8	8.1
San Bernardino	1989	1400	62.3	16.9	31.1	21.4	20.5	10.1
Santa Clara	3574	2641	73.9	13.7	31.6	28.7	20.0	6.1

Notes:
[1]Excluded from the totals are physicians classified as "inactive." Medical schools by county are: San Francisco (University of California, San Francisco); Los Angeles (University of California, Los Angeles, University of Southern California), Orange (University of California Irvine), Sacramento (University of California Davis), San Diego (University of California San Diego), San Bernardino (Loma Linda), and Santa Clara (Stanford).
[2]Includes office- and hospital-based physicians, but excludes residents and physicians involved in teaching, administration, research, and "other" activities.

Source: AMA Division of Survey and Data Resources, Physician Masterfile for 1983, September 1985. Table 11.

TABLE 6.5
Active Nonfederal Physicians by County as Percentage of GMENAC Standard for All Physicians, Primary Care Providers, and Surgical Specialists, 1983

County	All MDs			Active Primary Care MDs[1]			Active Surgical Specialists[2]		
	N	MDs/ 100,000	Supply as % of GMENAC Stand.[3]	N	MDs/ 100,000	Supply as % of GMENAC Stand.	N	MDs/ 100,000	Supply as % of GMENAC Stand.
Alameda	2,860	248.1	132.9%	1,018	144.9	169.9%	415	59.1	196.3%
Contra Costa	1,396	201.8	108.1%	439	63.5	74.4%	207	29.9	99.3%
Marin	887	397.9	213.1%	248	111.3	130.5%	112	50.2	166.8%
Napa	305	301.1	161.3%	93	91.8	107.6%	42	41.5	137.9%
San Francisco	4,421	629.1	337.0%	1,039	147.8	173.3%	495	70.4	233.9%
San Mateo	1,480	245.7	131.6%	475	78.9	92.5%	254	42.2	140.2%
Santa Clara	3,547	261.3	140.0%	1,145	84.3	98.8%	536	39.5	131.2%
Solano	305	121.3	64.9%	115	45.7	53.6%	43	17.1	56.8%
Sonoma	633	196.4	105.2%	281	87.2	102.2%	116	34.0	112.9%
GMENAC standard		186.7			85.3			30.1	

Notes:
[1] Primary Care includes General and Family Practice, Internal Medicine, Pediatrics, and Obstetrics/Gynocology.
[2] Surgical Specialties include General Surgery, Colon and Rectal Surgery, Neurological Surgery, Ophthalmology, Orthopedic Surgery, Otorhinolaryngology, Plastic Surgery, Thoracic Surgery, and Urology.
[3] Ratios based on GMENAC's projected supply requirements for 1990 using U.S. Census Bureau population projections.

Source: GMENAC standards from Selected Characteristics of Active Non-federal Physicians and Percent Distribution, California, Year-End Figures for 1975, 1979, and 1983, CMA.

TABLE 6.6
Per Capita Income by County, 1980

County	# Physicians	Revised 1980 Income, U.S. Census*			Bay Area Ranking	
		Per Capita Income	Median Household	Median Family	Per Capita	Median Family
San Francisco	641.6	9,265	15,866	20,911	5	9
Marin	375.6	12,332	24,554	29,721	1	1
Napa	301.7	8,503	18,887	22,426	7	6
Santa Clara	253.9	9,518	23,369	26,659	4	3
Alameda	237.9	8,537	18,700	22,863	6	5
San Mateo	218.7	10,666	23,172	27,279	2	2
Contra Costa	194.4	9,823	22,870	26,510	3	4
Sonoma	186.0	8,091	17,732	21,269	8	8
Solano	124.1	7,226	19,264	22,394	9	7
CALIFORNIA		8,295	18,243	21,537		

Notes: *Corrections for 1980 census questionnaires, as reported by the California State Census Data Center

Source: California State Census Data Center Newsletter 3 (4), Summer 1983, p. 3.

TABLE 6.7
Advertisements for Physician Placement, 1985, 1983, and 1977

County	Number of Advertisements		
	1985	1983	1977
San Francisco	2	2	10
Alameda	3	4	8
Contra Costa	1	6	7
Marin	1	3	1
San Mateo	2	1	2
Santa Clara	12	15	22
Total	21	31	50
Sacramento	6	6	9
Los Angeles	24	35	35
San Diego	3	7	12
Rural counties[1]	87	77	99
By Advertiser in San Francisco Bay Area:			
Health Maintenance Organization	0	0	9
County/State	0	1	2
Hospital	3	3	8
Group[2]	13	18	7
Small Group[3]	2	4	6
Solo Practice[4]	3	5	17
Community Health Center	0	0	1
Total	21	31	50

Notes:
[1]Rural counties include Alpine, Amador, Butte, Calaveras, Colusa Del Norte, El Dorado, Fresno, Glenn, Humboldt, Imperial, Inyo, Kern, Kings, Lake, Lassen, Madera, Mariposa, Mendocino, Merced, Modoc, Mono, Napa, Nevada, Placer, Plumas, San Joaquin, San Luis Obispo, Shasta, Sierra, Siskiyou, Solano, Sonoma, Sutter, Tehama, Trinity, Tulare, Toulumne, Yolo, and Yuba.
[2]"Group" includes practices with 10 or more members
[3]"Small group" includes practices with 3–9 members
[4]"Solo practice" includes practices for sale and those with 1 or 2 members

Source: Physician Placement Bulletin, November–December issue, 1977, 1983, 1985, CMA.

142

TABLE 6.8
Distribution of Participants in the Blue Cross Prudent Buyer Program and Crossover Between Prudent Buyer and Pru-Net Programs by Date of Graduation from Medical School

	Date of Graduation and Age				
	1975+ (under 35)	1965–1974 (35–44)	1955–1964 (45–54)	1945–1954 (55–64)	Before 1945 (65+)
San Francisco	24.0	34.1	24.8	11.0	6.1
Marin	12.1	42.4	34.8	7.6	3.0
Santa Clara	26.2	33.3	25.3	11.9	3.3
Crossover between Blue Cross and Pru-Net in San Francisco	19.3	37.9	27.1	12.1	3.6

TABLE 6.9
Medicare Participation Rates by Specialty, San Francisco County, for the Period of October 1984–September 1985

Specialty	# Listed*	% Participating Medicare
General practice	107	45.8
Family practice	24	62.5
Subtotal:	131	48.9
Medical specialties		
Allergy	10	40.0
Cardiovascular	47	36.2
Dermatology	50	54.0
Gastroenterology	9	55.6
Internal medicine	320	28.8
Nephrology	8	50.0
Pediatrics	1	0.0
Pulmonary disease	12	91.7
Subtotal:	457	32.9
Surgical specialties		
Cardiovascular	11	72.7
General Surgery	97	55.7
Neurosurgery	19	78.9
Obstetrics/gynecology	55	63.6
Ophthalmology	95	35.8
Orthopedic/hand	80	35.0
Otolaryngology	40	55.0
Plastic	13	69.2
Proctology	5	0.0
Subtotal:	415	49.4
Other		
Anesthesiology	52	3.9
Neurology	36	50.0
Nuclear Medicine	6	50.0
Pathology	11	54.0
Psychiatry	126	79.4
Radiology	35	5.7
Subtotal:	266	49.2
Information Missing	4	NA
Total:	1273	44.1

Notes: *Excludes physicians submitting fewer than 100 Medicare claims in 1983; also excluded are multiple physicians submitting claims under one identification number.

Source: San Francisco Medical Society (SFMS), from data compiled by Blue Shield of California, Medicare Participating Physician/Supplier Directory (MEDPARD), Calendar Year 1983.

TABLE 6.10
Medicare Assignment Rates, San Francisco County, 1982 and 1983

Rate of Participation[1]	1983 Claims					1982 Claims	
	Individual # Physicians	% Total	# SFMS Members	% Total	% of Individual MDs	Individual Physicians	% Total
Participating	563	44.2	363	40.2[2]	64.5	—	—
90–100%	86	6.8	36	4.0[2]	41.9	201	16.6
80–89	38	3.0	25	2.8	65.8	86	7.1
70–79	24	1.8	18	2.0	75.0	63	5.2
60–69	45	3.5	38	4.2	84.4	84	6.9
50–59	56	4.4	47	5.2	83.9	85	7.0
40–49	76	6.0	60	6.6	78.9	100	8.3
30–39	97	7.6	79	8.7	81.4	173	14.3
20–29	118	9.3	92	10.2	80.0	241	19.9
10–19	100	7.9	86	9.5	86.0	123	10.2
0–9	70	5.5	59	6.5	84.3	54	4.5
Total	1273	100.0	903	100.0	70.9	1210	100.0

For non-participating physicians, percentage	1983	1982
accepting assignment 50% of claims or more	19.5	42.8
accepting assignment 49% of claims or less	36.3	57.2
Medicare participating	44.2	—

Notes:
[1]Excluded from Medicare tabulation are physicians submitting fewer than 100 Medicare claims yearly, from 1982 and 1983.
[2]Indicates statistically significant difference between all physicians and SFMS members at the 95% confidence level.

Source: SFMS, Report of Chronic Illness and Aging Committee, p. 8, March 21, 1984 (1982 data); SFMS, Analysis of 1983 PARL List, December 1984 (1983 data).

TABLE 6.11
Medicare Assignment Rates, Selected Counties, 1983

County	Total #	0–9	10–19	20–29	30–39	40–49	50–59	60–69	70–79	80–89	90–100	Medicare Participating
ALAMEDA												
Internal Medicine	(224)	10.3%	14.7%	10.3%	7.6%	7.6%	3.6%	1.3%	1.8%	4.0%	3.6%	35.3%
Ophthalmology	(53)	5.7	11.3	20.8	9.4	5.7	5.7	1.9	1.9	1.9	—	35.8
Groups/clinics	(56)	—	1.8	1.8	—	3.6	1.8	1.8	—	—	28.6	60.7
MARIN												
Internal Medicine	(34)	20.6	32.4	20.6	14.7	—	2.9	—	—	2.9	—	5.9
Ophthalmology	(12)	8.3	33.3	25.0	16.7	8.3	—	—	—	—	—	8.3
Groups/clinics	(10)	10.0	20.0	10.0	10.0	10.0	—	—	—	—	10.0	30.0
SAN FRANCISCO												
Internal Medicine	(334)	6.6	10.8	9.3	8.4	9.0	5.4	6.3	3.0	5.4	3.6	32.3
Ophthalmology	(101)	9.9	14.9	14.9	7.9	1.0	4.0	2.0	—	—	8.9	36.6
Groups/clinics	(68)	—	—	1.5	2.9	—	—	—	4.4	2.9	26.5	61.8
SANTA CLARA												
Internal Medicine	(232)	19.0	22.8	10.8	8.2	4.7	1.7	0.4	0.9	0.9	11.2	19.4
Ophthalmology	(65)	12.3	24.6	18.5	13.8	4.6	1.5	3.1	—	1.5	1.5	18.5
Groups/clinics	(60)	5.0	3.3	5.0	3.3	3.3	—	—	5.0	1.7	21.7	51.7

Source: Physician/Supplier Assignment Rate List (PARL). Blue Shield of California. Calendar Year 1983 Medicare Program (Revised).

TABLE 6.12
Physician Income by Specialty and Medical Group, 1982–1986

Specialty	1982	1983	1984	1985	1986
INTERNAL MEDICINE					
Group A[1]	$48,900	$54,600	$58,800	$60,000	$60,000
Group B[1]					
w/o experience		50,000	55,000	115,000[2]	
with experience		65,000	62,000	50,000	
Group C				58,000	
Group D				54,444–66,170	
San Francisco City and County					
AMA average: Pacific Region[3]	85,300	90,100			
AMA average: U.S. <36[4]	63,100	68,000			
GENERAL SURGERY					
Group A	48,900	54,600	58,800	60,000	60,000
AMA average: Pacific Region	110,000	130,700			
AMA average: U.S. <36	91,500	108,800			
OBSTETRICS/GYNECOLOGY					
Group A	60,000	68,400	72,600	73,800	73,800
Group B	116,200			75,000	
Group C			60,000		
AMA average: Pacific Region	86,300	137,200			
AMA average: U.S. <36		78,900			
PEDIATRICS					
Group A	46,500	51,600	55,800	57,000	57,000
Group B		50,000		50,000	
Group C		42,500			
AMA average: Pacific Region	75,600	76,800			
AMA average: U.S. <36	59,400	44,700			

PSYCHIATRY					
Group A	49,800	54,900	58,800	60,000	60,000
Group B	70,100	79,500		60,000	
AMA average: Pacific Region	54,000	64,900			
AMA average: U.S. <36					
ANESTHESIOLOGY					
Group A	66,000	75,000	84,000	90,000	90,000
Group B	115,600	151,000		140,000	
AMA average: Pacific Region	110,700	126,900			
AMA average: U.S. <36					
ORTHOPEDICS					
Group A	69,000	78,000	84,000	96,000	96,600
Group B w/o experience	90,000	105,000	115,000		
OROLARYNGOLOGY					
Group A	60,000	69,000	75,000	76,200	76,200
Group B	72,000				
EMERGENCY ROOM[5]					
Group A	50,400	56,100	60,300	63,300	72,000
Group B				60,000	

Notes:
[1] Salaries quoted are without any bonus or profit sharing.
[2] Salary for faculty member (professor) at medical school.
[3] Mean physician net income after expenses, before taxes for Pacific Coast states.
[4] By physician age, without geographic breakdown (U.S. means).
[5] For physicians completing emergency medicine residency; must be board eligible.

Source: 1983–1984 AMA Socioeconomic System Core Survey, Table 38, in *Socioeconomic Characteristics of Medical Practice.*

7

Policy Directions

Eli Ginzberg

Dr. Frank Rhodes, the President of Cornell University, urged the members of the second Cornell Medical College Conference on Health Policy to move beyond diagnosis and to formulate directions for public policy. During the course of the five sessions, various policy proposals surfaced and were briefly discussed, and the conferees were afforded an opportunity in the closing session to discuss the proposed policy recommendations, which follow:

- A strong plea was made for a major reassessment of the "discipline of medicine" without which, it was contended, the curriculum of medical education could not be radically restructured and, it was agreed, this restructuring is long overdue. As first suggestions, the following three core elements of a restructuring were identified: the history and social role of medicine; its scientific basis; and the key analytic attitudes that should receive special emphasis. The restructured curriculum must be geared to the future and not constrained by the past.
- With so much of the medical system in flux, it is important, in fact it is essential, that a long-term planning process be established which will be capable of assessing the myriad changes that are under way and which will seek to monitor them so that the strengths of the extant system can be preserved while attempts are made to correct its shortcomings. It was recognized that a critical issue remains open: Who has the primary responsibility for taking the lead in assuring that such a longitudinal planning process will be initiated and continued?
- The conferees acknowledged that the medical educational system needs major restructuring and reform and advanced the proposition that it will be impossible to achieve the necessary reforms unless

attention is first directed to reforming the payment system for physicians. The present gross discrepancies in fee schedules have introduced such rigidities in the structure of medical education and health care delivery that successful reforms will require antecedent attention to the payment system.

- Since all aspects of the medical system are in flux, it was suggested that attention be centered on "damage control" particularly with regard to medical school applicants. They need to be forewarned about the immensity of the changes that are under way and those that are still to come; it is important to help those who are considering medicine as a career to develop realistic anticipations and thus avoid later regrets and frustrations.

- Several participants strongly wanted future medical students to cover all of their tuition costs by some combination of family assistance and loans. But these advocates recognized the desirability of assuring that students from low-income homes, especially those belonging to minority groups, be afforded significant financial assistance so that medicine did not become the career choice of an exclusively upper-income class.

- The elusive issue of foreign medical graduates (FMGs), those of either foreign or U.S. birth, was singled out as a subject that calls for early definitive action. It makes no sense in a period of growing physician supply to keep a back door open for less qualified and less prepared students.

- It was argued that the medical educational establishment should develop a consensus about the types of assistance it requires from the federal government and to speak with one voice to the Congress.

- The question was raised whether the title of the Conference which refers to a "patient shortage" is erroneous because there are so many underserved patients and whether the individual patient is necessarily the only unit. It was suggested that the family, the neighborhood, and the nation are also valid units of concern.

- Another issue raised was whether and to what extent the use of research funds for the financing of education have been dysfunctional and the potential advantages of seeking an independent basis for the future financing of education from tax revenue or other sources.

- It was emphasized that in all discussions about the changes under way on the health scene the consumer has a critical role. What medical services he or she wants will have a strong impact on the reshaping of the system.

- It was suggested that the central locus of medical care has begun to shift and will accelerate from hospitalization for acute illness among younger population groups to long-term care for the elderly and the importance of the hospital will diminish in favor of broad community service programs in which physicians will work with other health care providers from nurses to social workers.

- In assessing the reality of a present or prospective physician surplus it was emphasized that the changing contours of the health care system with its trend toward corporatization and related changes are creating opportunities for new careers in health management, medico-legal areas, wellness programs, and still other initiatives.

- The traditional internalization of all aspects of professional work can no longer be maintained. A more alert and concerned public will allow the medical profession to have wide margins for decision-making, but it will insist that it too have a role in matters of direct concern from learning about options of care to costs of care.

- Although conferees agreed that it is important for medicine to speak with one voice it was pointed out that there are basic differences among practitioners, directors of residency training programs, and department chairmen in medical schools and on many critical issues they would see a policy issue, such as the prospective surplus of physicians, from differing vantages.

- In the current changing environment, many events have downbeat or negative implications for one or another participating group. But in the large scheme of things it is far less important that the earnings of physicians are slipping than that the poor who need care are dropping between the cracks of a more constrained payment system.

- A strong case was advanced for leadership groups within both the medical profession and the business sector to focus on significant long-term issues such as how to provide mental health services, an increased focus on prevention, and the improvement of health status. While the current discussion is still heavily focused on controlling costs, basic value issues must be imbedded in the redesign of health policy.

- The point was made repeatedly that exclusive concern with cost containment to the disregard of quality makes no sense and that in matters of quality the medical profession must take the lead.

- In considering the future supply of physicians, allowances must be made for the following dimensions: the shift to ambulatory care; the growth of managed systems; the need for care created by new disease entities; and the role of future technology.

- In attempting to balance the supply of and demand for physicians, we must note that while the market is a potent force working for equilibrium, there are special areas where the market cannot provide satisfactory answers and alternative social mechanisms should be sought. An instance is the need to assure that people in low-income or isolated areas have access to health care.

- Surprise and distress were expressed with the statement that the academic health centers have been unable to take significant actions to help resolve the major problems confronting them. It was the consensus that this lack of response by the parties most directly concerned could only contribute to deepening their problems.
- The suggestion was advanced that a critical "reform lobby" be established to look at the present and prospective loosening of the extant health care system as an opportunity for long-delayed changes and that lobbyists outline the steps required to accomplish worthwhile reforms. Among the new opportunities are altered relations between physicians and other health care providers, particularly nurse practitioners, which might lead to greater patient satisfaction and lower costs.
- It was suggested that while the action of the federal government to expand the physician supply in the 1960s had been sound, it would be unwise for the federal government to move at present to constrict the supply. Many believe that current and future financial arrangements will price many prospective medical students out of the market and that this will lead to a reduction in the future supply of physicians. In a period of realignment, it is important to cut the costs of educating medical students, which on the average is based on a 1-to-1 faculty/student ratio.
- There is some danger in the "potential disenfranchisement" of the medical profession which suggests the need for new approaches to ensure that the medical profession will continue to have significant inputs into the reformulation of health care policy.
- The annual crop of new medical school graduates accounts for only about 3 percent of the active supply. It is good for physicians to develop lifestyles which include a shorter workweek, expanded opportunities for retraining, and, later, for reassessing the processess leading to retirement in order to make the transition more responsive to their individual needs.

The foregoing paragraphs provide a summary of the policy presentations and directions advanced by the conferees in the concluding session. The following is my personal interpretation of the policy issues that were identified by the writers, by the discussion sessions focused on each of the papers as well as the summary issues that have just been detailed. The paragraphs that follow are a shortened and somewhat sanitized version of the strong propositions which I advanced as the reasons why the Conference had encountered difficulties in addressing the policy challenge which Dr. Rhodes had posed in his charge.

With respect to the future flow of medical school applicants, Dr. Swanson's second forecast based on an 8 percent annual decline between 1986 and 1989 could result in an ominous situation, especially if the 8 percent proves to be too modest as well it might. If 8 percent or more is correct, medical schools will be unable to fill their classes with fully qualified applicants. These questions would then arise: Will the medical schools lower their standards to protect the jobs of their faculties? Will the public support a reduction in the entering class? Will legislators be able to close down the weakest medical schools? These are tough policy issues and they are just over the horizon.

It is difficult to understand why, after years of discussion, the medical leadership, representatives of the federal Administration, and state licensing boards have not been able to take definitive action to bring the FMG-USFMG issue under effective control. Although the flow of FMGs could not be cut off precipitously without endangering the medical service requirements of certain hospitals, the present flush supplies of U.S. physicians and specialists indicate that a controlled cutback could be achieved without serious disruption. The failure to act on this limited front is a poor augury for constructive medical policy initiatives.

Different analysts report many different estimates of the costs of educating medical students; many private schools insist that the annual outlay is in the neighborhood of $50,000 per student. Since the schools report a ratio of one faculty member to one undergraduate, the cost estimates appear reasonable. But there are problems. When the AMA asks physicians to identify their principal activities, a small number identify "teaching," a large number "research." Moreover, students complain of difficulties when they want to consult senior faculty. Finally, it is a common custom during the first two years of medical school instruction to subdivide basic courses among ten, twenty, or even more presenters and with no one person taking responsibility for integrating the materials. Dr. Rhodes warned the conferees in his introductory statement that it is not sensible to operate a medical school on a one-to-one ratio and that such a ratio can not long survive. The question now is, who will insist that changes be introduced? Until now deans have not been able to take the initiative; university presidents keep their distance from their medical schools; the departmental chairmen are more or less satisfied with the status quo. As a result, no significant changes have been instituted; some would say that no change has been introduced since the Flexner revolution of 1910!

There have been many discordant views over the past decades about the fields in which residents pursue primary care, specialty, or subspecialty training and in 1971 and again in 1976 Congress legislated to alter the outcomes. The many who opposed intervention to shift the distribution in favor of more primary care on the ground that it did not fit the preferences of physicians or patients were able to make a strong case. But recent data point to the necessity of reexamining the non-intervention approach on the ground that if specialists cannot perform their specialty for more than a limited number of hours per week, their skills will not remain honed and their patients will be at risk. The question of more or fewer specialists has become intertwined with issues of quality control.

Many leaders of U.S. medicine call attention to the erosion of physicians' incomes and the likely continuation of that trend. They fail to note, however, that in 1985 the average physician earned over $110,000 and the average surgeon, over $150,000. Moreover, they do not take account of the abnormal shifts that have occurred since the period prior to World War II when a physician earned about $5,000 and a full professor at a major university earned $7,500. No group in the United States has enjoyed a larger absolute and relative increase in earnings than physicians in the post–World War II decade. One of the most difficult problems which young physicians face is adjusting downward the earning expectations which they had when they selected medicine as a career.

Many believe that the payers of health care, particularly the federal and state governments and employers, are determined to constrain costs; in fact they believe that they are succeeding. In 1970, when the total spent for health care reached $75 billion, President Nixon warned about the excessive rate of increase in spending for health care and in 1985 after fifteen years of attempts at containment it had risen to $420 billion. Surely there is ground to question assumptions about both intent and capacity of payers to introduce effective cost containment. Congressmen will proceed deliberately before they move to cut back Medicare benefits for the elderly. And it is questionable, at least to me, that employers will risk the labor conflicts which might result from their going after larger "give-backs."

There are strong differences of opinion among well-informed persons about the extent to which the health care sector can rely on competition and the market to bring about optimal social results. The consumer is in a poor position to make professional judgments about competence and quality; about 40 million individuals have no coverage and additional millions have inadequate coverage; the future of medicine is closely tied to improvements in research and education. As a result, it is not clear, at least to this observer, that the market is a reliable mechanism for allocating dollars, personnel, or services. We have no option but to rely in large part on other mechanisms to assure that the system remains vibrant and progressive.

There is concern in the medical profession that the autonomy of the physician is being constrained and that economic considerations rather than the patient's well-being will determine treatment. But economic considerations were not absent in physician decision-making prior to Medicare and Medicaid and those considerations cannot be disregarded over the long run. But it is important to avoid a direct conflict of interest in the choices open to a physician in choosing a treatment plan. A physician should not be the direct beneficiary in deciding to withhold treatment any more than he should have decided on a course of treatment for his own economic benefit in earlier years. Moreover, while cookbook medicine is to be deprecated, the establishment of protocols are not inherently bad or dysfunctional to either patient or physician.

We must find a middle road which leads to a number of not easily reconcilable goals: the effective diagnosis and treatment of the patient; a satisfying professional environment for the physician; monitoring of access, quality, and cost of medical care; assuring that an increasingly educated population has an opportunity to participate in the decision-making which will affect alternative modes of treatment; and improved methods of identifying and controlling the work of ineffective physicians. It is simplistic to assume that physicians alone can achieve these important societal objectives. It is equally simplistic to believe that they can be achieved without the wholehearted and continuing participation of the physician community. The call here is for the leadership of the concerned groups, including government, to explore ways of making progress.

Despite many prognostications of the future health care system including forecasts that before long most Americans will be enrolled in HMOs or PPOs; that most physicians will be salaried employees; and that ten to twenty mega-corporations will control delivery of all health care services, a more cautionary view suggests that none of the foregoing gloomy forecasts is ordained or even likely. There will be a long shakedown period before the consumer opts for restricting his choices about modes of health care delivery. It appears highly unlikely that, in a high-income society in which consumers want to specify in great detail the colors and accessories of their cars, they will for a modest price differential barter away their freedom to pick their preferred physician. Some consumers may decide to reduce their freedom of choice for a cost advantage but it appears unlikely that this trade-off will ever dominate the system. It seems more likely that consumers will make different decisions about different providers, depending on the nature of the health service that they seek; physicians will work and earn their incomes from multiple sources; and it will be years before we will know which of the plethora of new providers can survive in a clearly more competitive market. Moreover, it seems unlikely that the survivors in one region will necessarily be the survivors in another. We should recall that HMOs, which penetrated the California market so early, until recently had little success in other regions of the country.

The many prophets, true or false, who are currently commanding the attention of the press and the public, are not seriously handicapped by facts and figures which would reveal the actual events in specific locations. As we have noted, California is not typical of the United States and neither is Texas, Florida, or New York. Consequently for the foreseeable future we will have to restrict generalizations both about what is happening and what is likely to happen. We have talked and talked during these last fifteen years about cost containment, but the most recent figures for 1985 show the widening gap between talk and reality. This should be a warning that as we become aware of the need to redouble our efforts to provide broader access for the poor and the near poor, as we seek to achieve some cost reductions and as the issue of quality comes to center stage, the crux of health care policy will move from dollars to basic values, a movement that will permit no easy, simple, or permanent answers.

About the Contributors

Eli Ginzberg, Ph.D., is director of Conservation of Human Resources; Hepburn Professor Emeritus of Economics at the Graduate School of Business; and director of the Revson Fellows Program, all at Columbia University.

Sandra S. Hunt, M.P.A., is policy analyst, Institute for Health Policy Studies, University of California, San Francisco.

Harold S. Luft, Ph.D., is professor of health economics, Institute for Health Policy Studies, University of California, San Francisco.

Stephen C. Schoenbaum, M.D., is deputy medical director for health practices, Harvard Community Health Plan, and associate professor of medicine, Harvard Medical School.

M. Roy Schwarz, M.D., is vice president, Medical Education and Science Policy, American Medical Association, and former dean, University of Colorado School of Medicine.

Rosemary A. Stevens, Ph.D., is professor of history and sociology of science, University of Pennsylvania.

August G. Swanson, M.D., is director, Department of Academic Affairs, Association of American Medical Colleges.

Joan B. Trauner, Ph.D., is assistant adjunct professor, Institute for Health Policy Studies, University of California, San Francisco.

Cornell University Medical College Second Conference on Health Policy

Conference Organizers

Thomas H. Meikle, Jr., M.D.
The Stephen and Suzanne Weiss
  Dean
Cornell University Medical
  College
New York, New York

Michael J. Sniffen
Executive Director
Cornell Health Policy Program
Cornell University Medical
  College
New York, New York

Conference Participants

John R. Ball
Associate Executive Vice
  President
American College of Physicians
Washington, D.C.

Mary Naylor
Chairman and Professor
Department of Nursing
Thomas Jefferson University
Philadelphia, Pennsylvania

Jon Christianson
Professor
University of Arizona
Tucson, Arizona

David Nexon
Minority Staff Director
U.S. Senate Labor, Human
  Resources Committee
Washington, D.C.

Donald R. Cohodes
Executive Director of Policy
Blue Cross Association
Chicago, Illinois

Elliot Roberts
Director
Charity Hospital of Louisiana
New Orleans, Louisiana

Lynn Etheredge
Senior Research Associate
The Urban Institute
Washington, D.C.

Paul Ginsburg
Senior Economist
The Rand Corporation
Washington, D.C.

Eli Ginzberg
Director
Conservation of Human
  Resources
Columbia University
New York, New York

Willis Goldbeck
Executive Director
Washington Business Group on
  Health
Washington, D.C.

Alfred Haynes
Dean
Charles R. Drew Post-graduate
  Medical School
Los Angeles, California

John Iglehart
Editor
Health Affairs
Millwood, Virginia

Harold S. Luft
Professor
Institute for Health Policy
  Studies
University of California
San Francisco, California

Hirsch Ruchlin
Professor of Economics in Public
  Health and Medicine
Cornell University Medical
  College
New York, New York

Tom Rundall
Robert Wood Johnson Health
  Policy Fellow
Washington, D.C.

Stephen C. Schoenbaum
Deputy Medical Director
The Harvard Community Health
  Plan
Boston, Massachusetts

Carl J. Schramm
Director, Center for Hospital
  Finance
Johns Hopkins University
Baltimore, Maryland

M. Roy Schwarz
Vice President for Medical
  Education & Scientific Policy
American Medical Association
Chicago, Illinois

Michael Soper
Senior Vice President
National Medical Management
Miami, Florida

Rosemary A. Stevens
Professor
Department of History and
  Sociology of Science
University of Pennsylvania
Philadelphia, Pennsylvania

Nelson J. Luria
Managing Director
Health Care Finance Department
Merrill Lynch Capital Markets
New York, New York

August G. Swanson
Director
Department of Academic Affairs
Association of American Medical
   Colleges
Washington, D.C.

Fred McKinney
Health Policy Center
Brandeis University
Waltham, Massachusetts

Joan B. Trauner
Institute for Health Policy
   Studies
University of California
San Francisco, California

Thomas J. Meikle, Jr.
The Stephen and Suzanne Weiss
   Dean
Cornell University Medical
   College
New York, New York

Mark Wallace
Senior Vice President
The Methodist Hospital
Houston, Texas

Gordon T. Moore
Director of Medical Education
The Harvard Community Health
   Plan
Boston, Massachusetts

Lowell Weiner
Medical Director
Group Health Plan of Southeast
   Michigan
Troy, Michigan

Gail Wilensky
Vice President
Project HOPE
Millwood, Virginia

Index